READING RESISTANCE

INTERSECTIONS OF RACE, GENDER AND CLASS

PARUL CHAUHAN

BlueRose ONE
Stories Matter
New Delhi • London

BLUEROSE PUBLISHERS
India | U.K.

For permissions requests or inquiries regarding this publication, please contact:

BLUEROSE PUBLISHERS
www.BlueRoseONE.com
info@bluerosepublishers.com
+91 8882 898 898
+4407342408967

ISBN: 978-93-6783-801-3

Cover Design: Aman Sharma
Typesetting: Pooja Sharma

First Edition: April 2025

Contents

Preface

The essence of African American literature lies in its power to explore the dominant issues pertaining to the existence of people of African descent living in America. While their writings reflect the culture, resilience and their day-to-day tribulations, the emphasis in their works always falls on the themes of racism, slavery and struggle for equality. The literature produced by African American writers brought the point of view of black Americans in the literary world by presenting their experiences.

The book depicts a comparative analysis of Lorraine Hansberry and Suzan-Lori Parks in view of their association with history and its rewriting/ re-presentation in the African American context through their works. It also investigates the key elements like identity, black pride and dignity and portrays how hope sustains the existence of the marginalized and how they are determined to fulfil their dream of having a congenial and prosperous life in the midst of the racial tensions of the particular era, where they are offered only subservient jobs, irrespective of their potential.

The book focuses on social exclusion on the basis of gender, race and class. It endeavours to foreground the issues of the right of women to control their own bodies and takes into account the issue of subjugation of African American women who are not pushed to the periphery by racism alone but also by sexist and class biases. Further, it focuses on Black women's endeavour to articulate and reclaim their lost identity which was deliberately erased.

Lorraine Hansberry and Suzan-Lori Parks played a dominant role in the evolution of Black aesthetics in a powerful way. They turn the mirror towards Blacks, showing self-awareness, authentic representation of Blacks in contrast to the negative stereotypes perpetuated by the Whites. Both the playwrights endeavoured and succeeded in interrogating the authenticity of the history crafted by the Whites by relocating the actual identity of Blacks through their works.

Acknowledgements

I wish to thank all those who have supported and encouraged me. I am deeply indebted to my mentor Professor Girija Sharma, Former Dean of Studies, Himachal Pradesh University for providing me constant guidance and encouragement. I shall always be thankful to her for her unwavering support and love.

I would like to record my special indebtedness to my loving mother Mrs. Prem Lata Chauhan and my sisters Shivani and Shivangi who have always been highly encouraging and have stood by me throughout. A special thanks to my husband Mr. Vinay Verma for his enduring support, cooperation and love that helped me complete my work.

Finally, I thank the Almighty for His blessings and the strength I could acquire to accomplish my work.

1
Introduction

> We have always been imagining ourselves.... We are the subjects of our own narrative, witnesses to and participants in our own experience, and, in no way coincidentally, in the experience with whom we have come in contact. We are not, in fact, "other." We are choices. (Morrison 170)

For many years, important markers in the history of Blacks in America had been deliberately ignored. Many significant events such as the Harlem Renaissance and similar voices of protest across America accompanied by black population from the south to the north including the antislavery movement were almost entirely erased from the history of the USA. The 1960s were an important period in America in this context, when many African Americans raised their voices against the persistent inequalities prevailing there at that point of time. Also, the literature produced by African American writers brought the point of view of black Americans in the literary world by presenting their experiences. The 1960s heralded not just their resistance but also an assertion for their identity through creative endeavour. It was not an easy task for them to establish themselves and seek recognition. After a lot of struggle, they succeeded in securing respectability and a place for themselves. African American literature is now recognized as one of the important segments of world literature.

For a long time, writings by African Americans were ignored or dismissed by western scholars. African Americans brought to the forefront the memories and traces of their rich culture and tradition as well as the pain and trauma of centuries:

> During the 17th, 18th and 19th centuries, unknown black bards, as James Weldon Johnson recounts, placed their lips to the sacred fire of poetry and created "sorrow songs" whose lyrics responded to the dehumanization of the world of chattel slavery, a world that in the end, reduced African Americans to three fifths other. (Samuels et al. iv)

Through their works, African American writers portrayed the picture of the troubled world. Songs like "Steal Away", "Swing Low Sweet Chariot", and "Motherless Child" threw some reflection on the state of that period. Gradually, the Blacks carved out a place for themselves in the western American culture and started believing that in order to advance in the world; the first thing is to be themselves, not somebody else. They have to be real, what they are, and not what Whites want them to be.

The essence of African American literature lies in its power to explore the dominant issues pertaining to the existence of people of African descent living in America. While their writings reflect the culture, resilience and their day-to-day tribulations, the emphasis in their works always falls on the themes of racism, slavery and struggle for equality. Generally, African American literature has its focus on what is the position and role of an African American within the larger frame of society and what it means to be a black American. Albert J. Raboteau observes that the African American literature "speaks to the deeper meaning of the African American presence in this nation. This presence has always been a test case of the nation's claims to freedom, democracy, equality, the inclusiveness of all" ("African-American Literature").

Movements like the Harlem Renaissance, the Civil Rights Movement and Black Arts Movement which took place in the United States played a vital role in providing recognition to the art and culture of the Blacks. Among all these movements, the Harlem Renaissance of 1920 is one of the most prominent and influential:

> The Harlem Movement is also called 'literary Garveyism'. Marcus Garvey puts his full efforts to make African Americans well aware of their African origin, something they had preferred to ignore for so long. (qtd. in Berghahn 118)

Garvey's passion for his origins did not translate into any significant intellectual endeavour, but he did make a sincere effort to spur the fellow Black Americans into action. This separated him from the intellectuals and writers of the Harlem Renaissance. Marcus Garvey motivated his mass movement Universal Negro Improvement Association (UNIA) with the motto, "Up you mighty race! You can accomplish what you will!" (qtd. in Samuels et al. 230). His main aim was to unite African peoples by making them realize that they share similar African roots, experiences and urged them to obtain freedom and equality. This movement gave a ray of hope to Blacks and exhorted them to make a change in their lives through arts and literature. It was not only a literary movement of poets, novelists, essayists, story writers but also of visual artists, actors, musicians and dancers. The movement was the outcome of political and historical events in America but it, in essence, showcased African Americans and their culture through literature. In *The Souls of Black Folk*, W.E.B. Du Bois writes:

> And so by faithful chance the Negro Folk song—the rhythmic cry of the slave–stands to-day not simply as the

> sole American music, but as the most beautiful expression of human experience born this side the seas . . . (I)t still remains as the singular spiritual heritage of the nation and greatest gift of the Negro people. (qtd. in Samuels et al. 229)

During this period numerous black artists produced classic works. Some of the eminent writers of the Harlem Renaissance were Zora Neale Hurston, Jean Toomer, Langston Hughes and Countee Cullen. At the heart of Americanism is the Declaration of Independence's Proclamation—"We hold these truths to be self-evident, that all men are created equal, that they are endowed by their Creator with certain unalienable Rights, that among these are Life, Liberty and pursuit of Happiness" (Taylor III 106). Harlem Movement showcased the lives of African Americans. It is also considered as a significant movement as far as the progress of black women playwrights is concerned. It focussed on both women centeredness and racial consciousness, while carving out a space for black women's theatre in an emerging theatre tradition. During Harlem Renaissance, African American women also got an opportunity to show their worth through their artistic creativity that had been virtually invisible before that. Thus, Harlem Renaissance, also known as New Negro Movement offered a view of the "Golden Age" of African American creative expression where men and women both had a significant role to play. The black women writers of the first half of the twentieth century set the foundation for the black women playwrights of the 1950s. Prominent among them were Lorraine Hansberry and Alice Childress. Elizabeth Brown-Guillory's books *Their Place on the Stage: Black Women Playwrights in America* and *Wines in the Wilderness: Plays by African American Women from the Harlem*

Renaissance to the Present throw light on the ethos of survival in black women's theatre.

The Harlem Renaissance gave a ray of hope to the African Americans to put forth their views to assert their independence and to gain recognition in mainstream America. Through the reflection of their past in literature, African Americans began to take pride in their heritage which helped them to grow. The writers expressed what they wanted to without any boundaries and restrictions. The three entirely different individuals associated with the movement namely Washington, Du Bois and Garvey came forward and participated profoundly in their own ways giving an unprecedented impetus to the movement:

> Whether it was Washington's model of slow progress and self provision, Du Bois' model of integration via intellectual advancement, or even Garvey's separatist nationalism, each man in his own way contributed a necessary element for the furtherance of the community. (Taylor III 114)

The Harlem Renaissance cannot be defined without acknowledging the role of Art. The Harlem Renaissance and the Black Arts Movement were inextricably connected, having more or less similar goals. After the Civil Rights Movement, Blacks were looking forward to a rebellion, which could lead to equality and self-empowerment. They wanted a radical change within the community. The main agenda of the Black Arts Movement was to turn around the negative/inferior images of African Americans portrayed in literature. In contrast to the Blacks' stereotypical representation by the Whites, the movement valorised African Americans and their culture. Drawing upon African American artistic heritage, these movements promoted the black artists by providing ample opportunities to them. They were encouraged to value their culture and traditions while being made aware of social disparities and their own marginality. The perspective whereby African Americans were represented in literature as criminals or misfits was strongly opposed by the exponents of these movements. They took the responsibility of creating a space for black creativity, bringing to the fore the needs and aspirations of the black people. The belief that it was necessary to acknowledge as well as to respond to the cultural needs of Blacks through the medium of their art, became their primary goal. Black Arts Movement encouraged black artistry by Blacks to establish their own press for publication houses. A number of black publishing houses, theatre troupes, and poetry readings groups appeared on the scene. Some significant magazines of the movement which in a way represented the ideology of the movement are *Liberator*, *Black Dialogue* and *The Journal of Black*. They focussed on re-exploration of western aesthetics and social responsibility of art. The movement brought into vogue a new style of language, creating new spellings, usage of pronunciation and avoiding capitalization in order to differentiate themselves from the western writers. The replacement of the world 'Negro' with 'Black' can be attributed to the Black Arts Movement solely. This movement exposed the domination of Blacks and focused on the idea of self-respect and identity of the Blacks. These artists used Black Nationalist or separatist themes in their works as they were aware that art and politics are inextricably linked. These writers and artists produced their works for the Blacks and they expected the critiques to come from the fellow black men and not from the Whites. The movement sought to express the viewpoint of Blacks, their pain and aspirations aiming to replace their conventional images in literature.

Larry Neal, one of the leaders of the Black Arts Movement makes a telling observation in this regard:

> The goal of black artist was to destroy the white way of looking at the world, eliminating white ideas from black art. . . For Black Art Movement artists, art had to be functional as well as beautiful. . . . The artist had a social responsibility for his/her art and its effect on the community. (qtd. in Smith-Spears 47)

During the course of the movement, new perspectives to African American expression were cultivated such as the use of African cultural references. The second half of the eighteenth century traced the earliest writings which had shown an interest in Africa, the continent, which had largely been absent from the imagination of the young Africans. It suddenly came to hold great fascination for the new generations of African Americans:

> African-Americans did become fascinated by Africa: they studied its culture, history, arts and languages. The identification with the African continent became so close that Africa and not America came to be often regarded as the real home of the American Blacks. (Berghahn vii)

Clarence Reed's 'Song from Wasteland' echoes this feeling powerfully:

> Africa, Africa Wrapped in sorrow
>
> Steeped in Pain
>
> Mother of us all
>
> I must home to the
>
> Warming womb
>
> From whence all sprang. . . . (qtd. in Berghahn vii)

Civil Rights Movement is also one of the most integral movements which played a vital role in building a platform for Blacks. The dominant genre of Civil Rights Movement literature is the memoir or personal autobiography. Looking back at the oral narratives and biographies of black women, one gets an insight into the lives of women who became part of desegregated schools. They took an active part in boycotts, taught in freedom schools and assisted locals in registering to vote. In the fight for civil rights, advocacy for equal participation of African American men and women in society was a major concern. African American women's fight for freedom was part of the Civil Rights Movement itself. The autobiographies that speak about women's movement are the most inspiring, compelling and unforgettable texts in African American literature.

The tradition of slavery had perpetuated racism in the white society. The Whites believed that it was their cultural legacy to treat Blacks unequally and exploit them. This system of racism which flourished in South America was named de Jure segregation, also referred as the Jim Crow system. The phrase de jure (by law) implied that the inferior status of African Americans and the superior status of Americans were reinforced by the legal code. It in a way justified the separation and differential treatment of Blacks and Whites. The Civil Rights Movement brought a momentous change by advocating equal advantages to the black Americans by raising a voice against the Jim Crow laws. Many people sacrificed their lives, went to prison, and marched in the streets in the expectations of assuring a better future for themselves and the generations to come. Though the famous leaders like Martin Luther and Jesse Jackson, who were associated with the movement, had worked hard for its success, it would not have been possible without the support and efforts of the ordinary people.

The true objectives of the movement could not have been achieved but for the black writers. The best known African American poets were Jupiter Hammon, Phillis Wheatley and George Moses Horton, all of whom were slaves but circumstances gave them a chance to express themselves through their poetry. Jupiter Hammon (1711-1806) was the first black American to publish poetry who lived in the historic Lloyd Manor house as a slave to Lloyd family all his life. He wrote religious folk poetry but his later prose espoused the freedom of Blacks. On September 24, 1786, he expressed his views on slavery in "Address to the Negroes of the state of New York," also known as "Hammon Address," before the African society, which contains his famous words, "If we should ever get to heaven, we shall find nobody to reproach us for being Black, or for being slaves" ("Jupiter Hammon Biography"). He advised the Africans not to bother much about their bondage as slaves. He held the view that slaves should do their work sincerely and be content with their lives. It is God's will that they are enslaved so they will never be reproached for their position.

In the middle of the nineteenth century, the genre which captured the attention of the people was the slave narratives. The main motive of this genre was to show a clear and true picture of the cruelties and hardships meted out to the slaves by their masters. It outlined how slaves were ill-treated and exploited by their masters. The word 'Sambo' had been used both in the American South as well the North to describe Blacks. Sambo was a plantation slave who was characterized as irresponsible, lazy, and easily given to lying and stealing. Whites defended slavery on the basis of racial difference. From their viewpoint, black people were fit for slavery as they were intellectually and morally inferior to Euro-Americans. According to Mercer and Julien, "Racism defined African peoples as having only bodies and no minds: Black men and women were seen as muscle machines and thus the super exploitation of slavery could be justified" (qtd. in Davies 54). All negative attributes were attached to the Blacks. It was assumed that due to the Blacks' lack of sense of responsibility, they were denied free existence. Following lines from *The Drinking Gourd* by Lorraine Hansberry depict the harshness of the rules made by the Whites for the Blacks: "You see, among other things there is no education to pay for— in fact, some of the harshest laws in the slave code are designed to keep the slave from being educated. The penalties are maiming or mutilation— or death" (170).

Slave narratives served as an enlightening element against the White's inhuman treatment of Blacks. Black men wrote of the barbarous cruelty of white punishment and dehumanization of black men. They brought to light their right to humanity. For male slaves, their masculinity was never in doubt rather white men were often afraid of their superior skills. But this was not the case with black women:

> For women, the struggle was twofold, as African-American women were not viewed as *women* but rather as female animals. The acquisition of literacy for blacks allowed female slaves the means to construct for themselves both their humanity and their womanhood. Slave narratives functioned as a testament to the suffering endured by female slaves at the hands of male and female masters. The dramatic cruelty of white women toward black women is one arcane element of slavery that female slave narratives exposed. (Beaulieu 796)

Slave narratives mainly aimed at exposing the evils of the southern plantations. The genre showcased the actual circumstances in the slaves' lives and emphasized the horrors of plantation life. It played a vital role in the fight against slavery by reiterating original accounts of brutal reality of the life of slaves. Slave narratives recount stories that reflect the authors' lives as slaves. There are many African American authors who have contributed to the above genre. The prominent writers of the slave narratives are Frederick Douglass, Olaudah Equiano and Linda Brent (Harriet Jacobs). These were the writers who were the actual witnesses to as well as the victims of the horrific and disgusting system of chattel slavery. The true meaning of freedom, the rights of the individuals, and universal human rights are the ideas echoed in their writings. Some of the important works of these writers are: *The Interesting Narrative and the Life of Olaudah Equiano* by Olaudah Equiano, *Narrative of Frederick Douglass, An American Slave, Written By Himself* by Frederick Douglass and *Incidents in the life of a Slave Girl, Written by Herself* by Jacobs. The earliest known slave narrative is that of James Albert Ukawasaw Gronniosaw: *A Narrative of the Most Remarkable Particulars in the life of James Albert Ukawsaw Gronniosaw, an African Prince, as Related by Himself* (1772). The book illustrates the beginning of both slavery and the slave narratives. Gronniosaw had dictated his story to a white Christian woman. The account paved way for other slave narratives to follow. And in addition, he added a preface which was also written by a white man. However, the first important slave narrative which served as an example of the genre and was written without any white collaboration was *The Interesting Narrative of the Life of Olaudah Equiano or Gustavus Vassa, the African, Written by Himself* by Equiano. Unlike Gronnioisaw, Equiano had penned his narrative himself as he was literate. The preface was written by himself and not by any white supporter. Though the writers of the slave narratives faced many hurdles but these narratives ultimately proved to be integral to both the larger African American literary canon and the American literary canon.

The narratives portray the slavery and predicament of black slaves very poignantly. They dig deep into the lives of the slaves and bring out the authentic experiences of the victims of slavery. The main aim of these writers was to bring legal and social change in society and to depict journey of a slave's struggle for survival and recognition. The black-white symbolism became a prominent theme of literature written during this period:

> Traditionally—and with little change to this day— this polarity is associated with a scale of values on which 'white' evokes predominantly positive responses, such as 'good', 'beautiful', 'pure', etc., whereas 'black' is invariably seen to be connected with 'bad', 'evil', 'night', 'mishap', 'ugliness', 'hell', etc. (Berghahn 4)

Historically, it was class, race and gender oppression which led to the suppression of the voices of black men and women. When ex-slaves were interviewed by white interviewers, they gave responses in white people's favour and chose slavery over freedom as they were scared of the brutal punishments and atrocities their masters were capable of meting out to them. Hence, they would only speak what Whites wanted to hear. The major reason behind this was the economic, political and social domination of the black people by the Whites. John Blassingame in his article, 'Using the Testimony of Ex- Slaves: Approaches and Problems' asserts:

> Many of the White WPA interviewers were ignorant in the ways of collecting oral histories, completely exercised white privilege in their interactions with the ex-slaves and were often blatantly condescending toward them. (qtd. in Young 60)

The ex-slaves were only comfortable with the black interviewers and talked to them in detail about the harsh treatment, poor food and housing, brutalities and even lynching of the Blacks by the Whites. White interviewers addressed black men and women as uncles, aunties, and mammies and sometimes even as niggers and darkies. And ex-slaves addressed them as masters and mistresses, clearly depicting the influence of the institution of slavery.

African American literature had got a fresh and new impetus as the stage was set for black American writers to get rewards which were denied to them before. For the first time attention began to be paid to the African American writers for their works, that for so long had been given to the Whites only. These black writers had continually progressed not only in one genre or field but in all the genres— drama, poetry and fiction. They were bestowed lots of prizes and awards which had added a charm to their creative endeavour. Gradually they were accepted in the canon of American literature and culture. Some of the prominent authors who made it possible were Langston Hughes, Richard Wright, Ralph Ellison, Toni Morrison, Zora Neale Hurston and Alice Walker. Langston Hughes was one of the most renowned writers of the renaissance. "*The Negro Speaks of Rivers*" is one of his most famous poems. Issues concerning racial segregation and Black Nationalism were raised by Richard Wright and Gwendolyn Brooks during the American Civil Rights Movement.

Native son (1940) is a novel by Richard Wright which was a great success. It dealt with the struggle of an African American for his acceptance in white society. Baldwin called Richard Wright "the greatest black writer in the world for me" ("African-American Literature").

There is an inherent connection between African American writing and Post colonialism. Post colonialism basically refers to a historical phase undergone by Third world countries after the decline of colonialism when countries in Asia, Africa and Latin America separated from the European empires and were left to rebuild themselves. Postcolonial theory deals with the writing by the postcolonial subject as resistance to colonial subjugation. It also focuses on literature by the colonized peoples of the erstwhile empire which attempts to articulate their identity and reclaim their past which was lost and deliberately erased:

> It has been suggested that it is more helpful to think of postcolonialism not just as coming literally after colonialism and signifying its demise, but more flexibly as the contestation of colonial domination and the legacies of colonialism. Such a position would allow us to include people geographically displaced by colonialism such as African Americans or people of Asian or Caribbean origin in Britain as 'postcolonial' subjects although they live within metropolitan cultures. It also allows us to incorporate the history of anti-colonial resistance with contemporary resistances to imperialism and to dominant Western culture. (Loomba 16)

Postcolonial theory probes the relationship between the centre and peripheries, the colonizers and the colonized. Racial superiority led the Whites to believe that the Blacks can work only as cheap labour and slaves. Later, the colonists developed a 'squatter system' which resulted in the bondage of Africans. This kind of system forced Blacks to become a labour power in exchange for living in European Land:

> Configurations such as 'colonial discourse analysis' insist upon the importance of studying literature together with history, politics, sociology and other art forms rather than in isolation from the multiple material and intellectual contexts which determine its production and reception. (Moore-Gilbert 8)

New Historicism presupposes that no text can be read independent of its social, historical and cultural context. Michael Warner phrases new historicism's motto as, "The text is historical, and history is textual" (qtd. in Guerin 283). According to Louis Montrose, new historicism focuses on 'textuality of history, the historicity of texts'. New Historicism purports to uphold both the identities of literature as well as history by focusing on their mutual establishment. Literature is not only an expression and reflection of historical acceptance but an inseparable part of a particular historical moment. Literature and history are interdisciplinary discourses which go hand in hand. It is impossible to present a history without the intervention of literature and in the same way literature also carries the mark of the historical context in which it was produced. Peter Barry defines:

> [N]ew Historicism is a method based on the parallel reading of literary and non-literary texts, usually of the same historical period. This is to say, new historicism refuses (at least ostensibly) to privilege the literary text: instead of a literary 'foreground' and a historical 'background' . . . (172)

New historicists believe that there is no distinction between literature and history. "They refuse to see literary texts against an overriding background of history or to see history as a set of facts outside the written text" (Brannigan 3). Any literary work is shaped by its social, cultural and historical background. Hence, it is unfair to evaluate a text without taking into account the historical perspective. New Historicism discards the autonomy of the text and the individuality of the writer, observing the view that the literary texts are inextricably intertwined to its historical milieu. As Hans Bertens states, "The role of the author is not completely negated, but it is a role that the author is at best only partially in command of. The author's role is to a large extent determined by historical circumstances." (176)

Black Feminism is an important aspect of the postcolonial theory and is integral to African American literature. It built up a literary tradition of empowerment. It dealt with the representations of the black women by the black women. Black feminist movement began with the premise that the black women were triply marginalized and oppressed. They realised that it is important to fight back by keeping in mind the multiple forms of oppression. It sought for the advancement of the status of black women in male and white dominant society. It became essential for them to deal with race, gender and class issues. In 1937, the National Black Feminist Organization came into being. Its purpose was to transform the image of black womanhood that was created by both male-dominated black liberation movement and by the white women's movement. Black women were relegated to the periphery by both the movements. White feminists had neglected and ignored the problems faced by poor and black women. And the Black Power Movement too had failed to recognize the issues specific to black women. During the 1970s, the black women responded to their lack of representation in a male dominated society. Black feminist thought leads to certain ideas that clarify a standpoint of and for the black women. Black feminist perspectives focus on the social domination on the basis of gender, race and class oppression. These oppressions are densely interwoven into social structures and work collectively to define the history of the lives of black women in America and other coloured women worldwide. They take us back to the era of slavery in the United States during which period, a societal hierarchy was established, according to which white men were supposed to be at the top, white women next, followed by black men and finally, at the bottom were placed black women. Black feminists were critical of the view that suggests that black women must identify themselves as either black or women.

Now, however, after centuries of oblivion, African American women writers occupy a central and abiding place in contemporary literature. They grew exponentially as major voices in the canon of African American literature. Their writings were not confined to the issues of racism, identity or colour but women's roles and representations, community, sexism and motherhood as well. Similarly, their preoccupation with the supernatural and the spiritual issues is also evident in their oeuvre. Suffering and silencing were the central themes found in black women's works as they vociferously articulated the triple burden of class, gender and race. As Lorraine Bethel comments:

> The codification of blackness and femaleness by whites and males is seen in terms of thinking like a woman and acting like a nigger which are based on the premise that these are typically black and female ways of acting and thinking. Therefore, the most pejorative concept in the white/ male

> world view would be that of thinking and acting like a nigger woman. (qtd. in Wisker 37)

Gay Wilentz and Lorraine Bethel have further commented on the suppression of African and African American women writing:

> The history of Black women's literature started long before Black women were finally allowed their right to literacy. Their literature and other creative art were oral, rooted in storytelling and the African-American folk tradition. (qtd. in Wisker 131)

Among the oldest known works of literature by an African American woman is a poem "Bars Fight" written in 1746 and authored by Lucy Terry (1730-1821). Other notable black women writers are Phillis Wheatley, Zora Neale Hurston, Margaret Walker, Toni Morrison, Alice Walker, Maya Angelou, Gwendolyn Brooks, Lorraine Hansberry and Suzan-Lori Parks. Gwendolyn Brooks became the first African-American to win the Pulitzer Prize for her 1949 book of poetry, *Annie Allen*. Her poetry was for ordinary people. Her major anthologies are *A Street in Bronzeville* (1946) and *The Bean Eaters* (1956), which made her famous.

One of the major voices in black writing is Toni Morrison. Her works dealt particularly with black people's lives and history. Her novels refer to the major issues like racism, slavery, quest for identity and so on. Toni Morrison was the first African American to be awarded the prestigious Nobel Prize in literature. She earned respect for black women writers through her substantial literary works which include *Sula*, *Beloved*, *The Bluest eye* and *Songs of Solomon*. For *Beloved* she won the Pulitzer Prize in

1988. Maya Angelou was also one of the well-known writers of African American literature. She was the first black female streetcar conductor in San Francisco. Her book, *I Know Why the Caged Bird Sings* is an autobiography which was nominated for the National Book Award and won popular and critical claim. Themes of racism, motherhood and freedom are integral to her works.

Another eminent writer belonging to this genre is Alice Walker. Her contribution in expanding and enriching African American literature as a whole and black women's writing in particular is immense. Alice Walker's involvement in voter registration drives, campaigns for welfare rights and children's programs reflect her active participation in the Civil Rights Movement. The main focus in her works is on the relationships between black men and women, family members and their community, southern culture and folklore. The idea of womanism is given in her collection *In Search of Our Mothers' Gardens* (1983) in which she defines the concept of 'womanism.' To Walker, a womanist is "[c]ommited to the survival and wholeness of entire people, male and female" (xi). Womanists' main concern seems to unify African Americans on the basis of the same struggle and history of suffering under slavery. Womanism celebrates black women's identity including the roles of a mother and a wife. Womanism is different from white feminism in the sense that some issues affecting black women are not touched upon by white feminism. Womanists give priority to family and work for the empowerment of family while a majority of white feminists view motherhood and the role of wife as subordinate and unfulfilling. Womanist belief is that motherhood is an integral part of women's life. Alice Walker examines the theme of motherhood in her essay,

In Search of Our Mothers' Gardens profoundly and writes about her own mother:

> [M]y mother adorned with flowers whatever shabby house we were forced to live in. . . . Whatever she planted grew as if by magic, and her fame as a grower of flowers . . . Because of her creativity with her flowers, even my memories of poverty are seen through a screen of blooms — sunflowers, petunias, roses . . . and on and on. (241)

Among the distinguished works by Alice Walker is *The Color Purple* which became a best-seller and received the National Book Award in 1983 and also fetched a Pulitzer Prize. In her seminal essay, *In Search of Our Mothers' Gardens,* she goes back to the era of her grandmother and mother, the days when reading and writing for black women was out of reach and was considered punishable. She explored and realized how the black women had suppressed their feelings, creativity and talent. There were so many hurdles in their way which hindered them from becoming artists, poets, novelists or dramatists. They were not understood by anyone and their deep agonies of not being heard and appreciated for anything they did, were buried with them as they died.

In the field of drama also, African American women created a place for themselves. It is considered that Angelina Weld Grimke's *Rachel* (1916) was the first play by an African American woman, which was produced publicly. In 1926, in Harlem a theatre named Krigwa Players Little Negro Theatre was started by W.E.B. Du Bois. Those days plays written by women appeared in churches and schools. Gradually women emerged as the strength of African American drama and their plays began to be performed frequently.

Lorraine Hansberry and Suzan-Lori Parks are two prominent names which can be added to the string of black women writers in African American literature. Their plays follow the struggle of African Americans against the colonial rule and address themes like racism, black feminism, masculinity, Africanism, quest for identity and dignity. While exploring the main issues related to racism and feminism, they have made efforts to bring to the forefront the African American women's triple marginalization. They challenge the male and white hegemonic structures which have subjugated the black women and encourage their women characters to think for themselves and fulfil their wishes by realizing their social existence which had been ignored due to hierarchical oppression. They believe that black women need to stand shoulder to shoulder in the struggle for equality; otherwise, their efforts would prove to be futile. They emphasize on how the bond of trust and cooperation among African American men and African American women can help them to attain liberty. Both the writers portray African American women as self-confident, socializing, courageous and acting responsibly as equally active participants in standing firm for freedom and in fighting against racial oppression. Their oeuvre mainly deals with representations of Blacks in American society. Both the writers mirror the passionate nature of African Americans through retaliation and assertion. By paying attention to the history and African American identity, they valorise the rich African culture in their works.

Lorraine Vivian Hansberry was a prominent African American dramatist. She has enriched the black women writing by her plays, especially her outstanding and award-winning play *A Raisin in the Sun*. It was produced in 1959 and was awarded the New York Drama Critics Circle Award. It was hailed as a watershed in the history of American drama. *A Raisin in the Sun* ran 530 performances. During the time when it was considered as the era of male playwrights like Eugene O'Neil, Thornton Wilder, and Tennessee Williams—Lorraine Hansberry appeared as a radical dramatist and paved the way for other black women dramatists to write fearlessly.

Born on May 19, 1930, Lorraine Vivian Hansberry was raised in Chicago in a family with social and intellectual advantages. Nannie Perry Hansberry, her mother was a teacher and a ward committee woman, and her father Carl. A. Hansberry was a US deputy Marshall and contributed immensely to the cause of social justice. He was active in the National Association for the Advancement of Colored People (NAACP). Carl. A. Hansberry had four children and Lorraine was the youngest. Major figures of black American culture and politics as W.E.B. Du Bois, Duke Ellington, Langston Hughes and Paul Robeson used to visit Hansberry's home when Lorraine was a child. Although Lorraine Hansberry had a sound family background, she always felt the trauma of oppression faced by the black Americans before the civil rights legislation of the 1960s. She had always wanted to be like her other friends. "Black" was the word handwritten on Lorraine Hansberry's birth certificate on May 19, 1930 but it was only after her parents asserted the right to designate their child's racial identity on their own terms. It was part of her life to challenge the unacceptable system. When she was eight years old, their family moved to Hyde Park, an affluent, all white neighbourhood. Carl Hansberry had to face many problems and many trials. Although the Supreme Court gave a decision in his favour and he won the case that was a hollow victory. The Hansberry family still remained victims of the hostility of the white people. All these instances affected Lorraine Hansberry very deeply.

Lorraine Hansberry attended the University of Wisconsin, Madison, a large and mostly white institution, for two years. She was also the President of the Young Progressive Association, national left wing student organization. Hansberry attended classes at the New York School for Social Research. She was involved in freelance writing and did odd jobs to sustain herself. Later she was hired by Paul Robeson, publisher of the progressive magazine *Freedom* and very soon got the rank of Associate Editor. But her profession as a writer never diminished her passion for social justice; instead, it intensified her activism for social causes more. She fought for human rights. Lorraine Hansberry got married in 1953 to Robert Nemiroff whom she met in June of 1952, while they were both protesting against the segregated Sports teams at New York University. Nemiroff was a graduate in literature and was from Russian-Jewish background. A day before their wedding, they marched in front of the Chicago Federal Building to protest against the imminent execution of Ethel and Julius Rosenberg. She always saw her identity as linked to her race and gender: "I was born black and a female." Lorraine Hansberry was born and brought up in a household where serious social commitment was instilled in the children. In her house, there was a fine library containing world classics and works by and about black people which resulted in the growth of Hansberry as a cultural catalyst for black social life in Chicago, a feature reflected in her plays.

Hansberry wrote about twenty articles for *Freedom* during her five-year association with the magazine and she focused her work on the issues of educational problems faced by Blacks and also on women's discrimination and racial issues. She worked to support the family but in 1956, Nemiroff achieved financial security and made a name for himself by writing the hit song "Cindy, Oh, Cindy," which was an instant success. Thereafter, Hansberry did not have to do odd jobs any longer and began to devote herself to full time writing. She also quit her job with the newspaper *Freedom*; she began to give maximum time to creative writing and thinking. Lorraine Hansberry made her debut at Broadway with *A Raisin in the Sun* (1959). She was the first black playwright and the youngest playwright to win the New York Drama Critics Circle Award. With the superb success of *A Raisin in the Sun*, Black American drama reached a new milestone. Hansberry took the title of the play from Langston Hughes' poem "Harlem":

> What happens to a dream deferred?
>
> Does it dry up
>
> Like a raisin in the sun?
>
> Or fester like a sore–
>
> And then run?
>
> Does it stink like rotten meat?
>
> Or crust and sugar over–
>
> Like a syrupy sweet?
>
> Maybe it just sags
>
> Like a heavy load.
>
> Or does it explode? (qtd. in Hansberry 3)

It dealt with the theme of racism mainly but it also threw light on some other important issues which are inescapable such as the value system of the black families; concepts of African American beauty and identity; class and generational conflicts and man-woman relationship.

Very few African American playwrights had been able to authentically portray the reality of black people's lives before Hansberry. Her drama powerfully reflected the predicament of black people's lives. Before she appeared on the literary scene as a playwright, she had highlighted in her writings, the major events in Africa, touching upon the social issues, problems faced by black ghetto students and women's protest against discrimination. At the public rallies she would raise a voice of protest against the prejudices of American society. The power of her language would keep her audiences and readers spell bound. Similarly, her theatre is also a theatre of protest. She invented real characters whom one could relate to. Speaking directly from the heart, her personal experiences of brutality and hostility at the hands of white community were reflected in her works. On the cover page of *A Raisin in the Sun*, the publisher quotes from the *New York Daily News*: "Hansberry, like the great Bernard Shaw, knew how to make provocative characters become real people on the stage . . . representing a variety of viewpoints on a subject of overwhelming importance" (Cover copy).

At an early age, Lorraine Hansberry had developed an interest in theatre. Production of Howard Richardson and William Berney's *Dark of the Moon* had fascinated Hansberry a lot. At Wisconsin, she became acquainted with the social drama. She was impressed by the plays by some eminent playwrights like Ibsen and Sean O'Casey. Particularly, *Juno and the Peacock* enchanted her most profoundly. After watching this play, she realized the importance and the power of theatre. She started believing that the true and the most appropriate way of conveying the experiences of real human life was through drama, which was the most powerful medium compared to any other literary form. Hansberry aimed at addressing social and political issues through her plays: "She did not believe that a sharp dichotomy exists between art and the propagation of ideas. She frequently asserted that all plays have a message . . . " (Carter 15). For years she struggled with her writing. In 1956, Hansberry had begun putting her efforts to work on a play, which portrays the struggle of a black family. She became the first black female playwright whose work was produced on Broadway. In October, 1964, Hansberry was struck by pancreatic cancer. At the same time Hansberry and Nemiroff divorced each other, but the end of marriage was not the end of their relationship. It did not in any way diminish their friendship. They remained good friends and work partners. After Lorraine Hansberry's death at the tragically early age of thirty-four, Nemiroff published her finished and unfinished works posthumously.

Some of the important works by Lorraine Hansberry are her collected last plays including *Les Blancs, The Drinking Gourd* and *What Use are Flowers?* Other plays include *A Raisin in the Sun, The Sidney Brustein's Window* and *To Be Young, Gifted and Black*. All her works made a great contribution to African American literature. *The Drinking Gourd* became the first play to be written for television. In this play Lorraine Hansberry brought out the essential view of "the realities of the time,"—particularly of slavery:

> Interestingly, it took its title from a spiritual, a song of the Underground Railroad which derived, in turn, from the old slave metaphor for the Big Dipper which points to the

> North Star, the symbol and beacon to freedom for many an escaped slave seeking its way North in the Southern night. (qtd. in Hansberry 149)

Through this play Lorraine Hansberry has depicted very vividly the cruelty perpetrated on the African American slaves. The motive of depicting all this is not only to criticize and condemn the Whites and their inhumanity but also to expose the pathetic system that promoted crime. There is a very touching scene where an innocent black boy is blinded by the white master just because of the statutory 'crime' of learning to read.

Hansberry had closely seen racism in American society and its effects on black Americans, the deprivation, ignorance and injustice faced by black people, man-woman relationship and self-determination of African countries. Hansberry's oeuvre is marked with realism. Since she wrote for the general theatre audience, her interest lies in dealing with the lives of ordinary people. Her language is colloquial.

During the life span of just 34 years, Lorraine Vivian Hansberry touched the heights of success and contributed immensely to the literary treasure of African American literature. Had she been alive she would have produced more literary works. Remarkably, however, Hansberry's death did not mark the end of her career as a dramatist. Her former husband Robert Nemiroff was designated her executor and proceeded to pull together and produce plays based on her works in progress and her other writings.

The other writer is Suzan-Lori Parks who is also an African American playwright, screenwriter and novelist. She is credited with the transfiguration of the American theatre through her mythic plays. She is the first African American who won the Pulitzer Prize for her play *Topdog/Underdog* and was the first to receive the Master Writer Chair at New York's prestigious Public Theatre. Born on May 10, 1963 in Fort Knox, Kentucky, Parks grew up in several different places owing to her father's career as an army colonel. She spent part of her childhood in Germany. While living in Germany she attended German High School instead of the American schools for the Children of military personal. This experience made Parks aware of what it feels like to be neither White nor Black, but simply foreign. While in school, Parks would write poems and songs with her brother. She also created a newspaper called "Daily Daily". After returning from Germany, she attended Mount Holyoke College, a women's liberal arts college, and studied under the renowned author and essayist James Baldwin, who encouraged her to become a playwright. He predicted that she may become one of the most valuable artists of their time. And later she indeed became one of the most significant and distinguished playwrights of America. Baldwin recognized her capability and potential to write plays. While still an apprentice, she began writing "*The Sinner's Place*," which became her senior thesis work. The English department awarded the play honours and Parks graduated in 1985 with B.A. in English and German literature. Parks began to take classes with Baldwin and at his suggestion started writing plays. She was also inspired by Wendy Wasserstein, a Mount Holyoke graduate who won the Pulitzer Prize in 1989 for her play *The Heidi Chronicles*.

Parks has a unique approach towards dramatic productions which has led her to emerge as a distinctive dramatist. She has been credited with changing the face of theatre by defying the linear and the static way of writing. In her essay, "From Elements of Style," she expresses her views:

> The naturalism of Lorraine Hansberry is beautiful and should not be dismissed simply because it's naturalism. We should understand that realism, like other movements in other art forms, is a specific response to a certain historical climate. I don't explode the form because I find traditional plays "boring"— I don't really. It's just that those structures never could accommodate the figures which take up residence inside me. (8)

Rejecting the naturalism of earlier drama and traditional linear narrative with a desire to create a new type of theatre, Parks chooses jazz to express the untold stories and feelings of the Blacks. By subverting the patriarchal forms and language in contemporary drama, Parks stands with her creation of an original dramaturgical technique that she calls "repetition and revision" or "rep and rev" which is one of the most important artistic skills of hers. She explains "rep & rev" as a concept related to jazz aesthetics in which a composer writes a musical phrase once and repeats it time and again with a revision each time. She often utilizes the African American dialect to render and unveil the hidden message behind the dialogues of her characters. The phrases in her plays are repetitive with little variations. In *The Death of the Last Black Man in the Whole Entire World*, the phrase, 'This is the death of the last black man in the whole entire world' is repeated many times with a bit of revision: "Yesterday today next summer tomorrow just uh moment uhgoh in 1317 dieded thuh last black man in thuh whole entire world" (102). This refrain reflects upon the Blacks' history of racial discrimination and violence. She describes her plays in terms of

"Rep & Rev" throughout her canon, be it the form or dialogues of her plays. Like jazz, there is repetition and revision in Parks' *The America Play*, in which Parks presents past with a revision. She rewrites the assassination of Abraham Lincoln but revises the past as Lincoln in her play is Black and not White. Rep. & Rev. is further clearly observed in her play, *The Death of the Last Black Man in the Whole Entire World.* The Black Man is considered as a revision of a figure of African American folklore, who comes back again and again. Parks here depicts as to how the past events haunt the present. Parks argues, "[T]he idea of Repetition and Revision is an integral part of the African and American literary and oral tradition" (10).

Her initial plays were completely experimental. They were not accepted for production due to their innovative form but it didn't discourage Parks and she continued to write in a way that permits her to represent her art and creation differently and unconventionally. Her oeuvre is varied in terms of form, style, and the subject matter. The exploration of works by African American playwrights Adrienne Kennedy and Ntozake Shange were key figures in the development of her art form. They both provided a more individualistic form of writing for Parks, who was looking to tell her stories in her own way which would not be structured by the confines of the traditional drama. Form and content, both are integral to her dramatic style. She discards the contemporary drama for ignoring the form just for the sake of message and emotional effect. Parks has asserted, "As a playwright I try to do many things: explore the form, ask questions, make a good show, tell a good story, and ask more questions, take nothing for granted" (qtd. in Larson 7).

Parks' great accomplishments in her life prove her genius. Shortly after graduating from Mt. Holyoke College in 1985, she studied acting for a year at Drama Studio in London in order to improve her writing. Besides, she is an outstanding and an engaging public speaker and lecturer. She is quite popular for her live performances in college campuses and before theatre audiences nationwide. Her passion for writing and her lectures have made her a highly respected teacher at the California Institute.

Suzan-Lori Parks has been a strong force in the African American tradition and is mostly recognized for the way she experiments with and explores language and dialects. Her works are complex and brilliantly experimental. "Parks' language is a performance, a spectacle for the eye as well as the ear. In fact, one of her greatest achievements is making the visual and verbal work together" (Kolin 16). She has invented a new stage language where her characters speak an African American vernacular. Not only is her technique brilliant, but her subject matter is also extremely relevant in that it challenges the accepted notions of American history. She has tried and in fact succeeded in creating and rewriting history through her works. "The historically focused elements of Parks' aesthetic position her as an author whose work challenges the ways readers imagine and experience history and/or receive recorded accounts thereof" (Larson 2).

Parks has also written mythic plays about black history and identity in contemporary America. She has very well captured the nightmares and horrors of African Americans and in a way exposed the white establishment which was bent upon erasing their history and wiping out their dreams. Through her plays, she poses a series of questions on issues like black cultural memory and black identity. While resisting white exclusionary history, Parks writes about the racial assaults directed against the black body and spirit. Her plays have significantly transformed the black American theatre. "With the post-colonial fervor, Parks portrays blackness as a symbol of subjugation, but even as she deconstructs the fantasies of power, she converts the black body into a theatre of trauma" (Kolin10). She digs deep and searches for an ancestral past of Blacks, lost somewhere in the course of history. Parks attempts to powerfully delineate racial identities of her characters in the play. She believes that being a dramatist it is her job to locate the past that has been almost forgotten. This is evident from her play, *Imperceptible Mutabilities in the Third Kingdom*, where the characters are not able to find their names and identities in order to restore their sense of self and dignity. Through the portrait of one of the main characters in the play, Parks has portrayed the plight and the divided selves of slaves. Kin-seer does not even recognize himself or his self until the over-seer, the one who represents the other world or the white world, assures him of his identity.

Parks can be categorized among those authors who try to put in place the absent or the neglected groups by revising the history and facts about it. She tries to rewrite history through the medium of her literary works that tend to bring to the forefront the fact that the texts, cultural events and figures affect an individual's racial identity. Her works challenge the imagination, acceptance and experience of history by the readers. Parks' texts represent the relationship of history and identity by revisiting and revising some of the most prominent texts and contexts in black history. They include Harriet Jacob's *Incidents in the life of a Slave Girl* (1861), the exploitation of the woman known as Venus Hottentot and Abraham Lincoln's assassination.

A powerful literary figure, Suzan-Lori Parks has contributed immensely to the canon of African American writing. Besides drama, her corpus also includes fiction and non-fiction. Her plays include *Imperceptible Mutabilities in the Third kingdom, Betting on the Dust Commander, The Death of the Last Man in the Whole Entire World, Pickling, Devotees in the Garden of Love, The America Play, Venus, In the Blood, Fucking A, Topdog/ Underdog, 365Days/365 plays, Father Comes Home from the Wars* and *The book of Grace*. She has written three essays "Possession", "From Elements of Style" and "An equation for Black People Onstage" and two screenplays *Girl 6* and *Their Eyes Were Watching God* which was an adaptation of Zora Neale Hurston's novel of the same title.

Suzan-Lori Parks has been conferred myriad honours in her literary career. She won a Pulitzer Prize for *Topdog/Underdog* in 2002 and became the first black woman to receive the honour for Drama. Her play *Imperceptible Mutabilities in the Third Kingdom*, won Parks the Obie award. She won another Obie Award for her play *Venus*. Her play *In the Blood*, was nominated for the Pulitzer Prize. In 2000, she received a Guggenheim Fellowship, and in 2001 she was awarded a MacArthur Foundation "Genius" Grant.

Lorraine Hansberry and Suzan-Lori Parks belong to different periods of the twentieth century and yet have striking similarities in terms of their forthrightness and a fearless portrayal of the lives of the African Americans. What Hansberry achieved through her writings living in a more hostile society is being carried further by Parks as she uncompromisingly lays bare those unavoidable truths of the sordid past of American history that dehumanised a whole populace owing to their race.

This book defines the similarities, dissimilarities and points of contact between Lorraine Hansberry and Suzan-Lori Parks. Rey Chow in her article defines, "Comparative Literature as a "Discipline of Tolerance," that is a loose discourse network sprouting from an incessant proliferation, intermingling and hybridization of subjects" (qtd. in Behdad and Thomas 4). The overall view of literature is very vast which could be differentiated on the basis of the social, political, economic, historical, racial, cultural and other influences. ". . . Comparative literature involves the study of texts across cultures, that it is interdisciplinary and that it is concerned with patterns of connection in literatures across both time and space" (Bassnett 1). The theatre of Lorraine Hansberry and Suzan-Lori Parks is the theatre of protest. In 1959, Lorraine Hansberry became the first and the youngest playwright to win New York Drama Critics Circle Award, while Suzan-Lori Parks became the first black playwright to win a Pulitzer Prize in drama. Parks draws attention to racism and black feminism as powerfully as Hansberry did in a very hostile social set-up. The presence of similar themes like racism, black feminism, slavery, retaliation and assertion become a powerful common link between the two writers. The recurrence of similar themes in both the playwrights' works depicts the universality of African Americans' experience over a period of time.

Themes of racism and slavery are demonstrated with their devastating effects upon the black psyche by both the playwrights. They have depicted the racial assaults and the many-sidedness of the saga of oppression, deep agony and brutality experienced by the Blacks. In *The Drinking Gourd,* Hansberry brings out the essential view of "realities of the time," of slavery. The tyranny of Whites is revealed throughout the play. Similarly in *Imperceptible*

Mutabilities in the Third Kingdom, Parks has depicted the slave's nightmares and their exploitation at the hands of Whites.

Hansberry and Parks have explored the issues related to feminism which remain prominent in their philosophy and works. They have highlighted the plight of black women and their marginalization. Their contribution to the revolutionary black theatre is noteworthy as they set forth the ideas of liberation of black men and women creating strong women characters. Lorraine and Parks have depicted black female identities in a radical manner. Their women are strong and courageous. They have reflected through their works the experience of having a black body and the consequent oppression faced by black women. Lorraine Hansberry bestows a certain dignity to her women characters. Motherhood is especially portrayed as the most sacrificing, self-denying and full of struggle. Her lifelike characters like Ruth Younger and Lena Younger reflect these attributes in *A Raisin in the Sun* and the slave mother Rissa in the posthumously published work *The Drinking Gourd* epitomizes motherhood. Her female characters are presented as robust with their self-affirmation and determination. They are depicted as headstrong as the male characters. Margaret B. Wilkerson says:

> Hansberry's "sighted eyes" forced her to confront fully the depravity, cruelty, and utter foolishness of men's actions, but her "feeling heart" would not allow her to lose faith in humanity's potential for overcoming its own barbarity. This strong and uncompromising belief in the future of humankind informed her plays and sometimes infuriated her critics. (qtd. in Bloom 79)

Hansberry made a huge contribution to the revolutionary black theatre. *A Raisin in the Sun* by Lorraine Hansberry opened up the issue of the rights of women to control their own bodies and their intellectual independence. Beneatha has an independent feminist perspective which is reflected by the assertive stand taken by her. She stands by what she believes in, challenging what the society thinks. The critic Rachelle S. Gold describes her complexity: "She is a budding feminist, educated, knowledgeable about her African heritage, sceptical about religion's role as a pacifying force and sensitive to how class barriers restrict her from certain social relationships" (qtd. in Bloom 2). Rissa makes a gesture of defiance against the system of slavery and black stereotyping by turning her back on her dying master.

Likewise, Suzan-Lori Parks' plays showcase the plight and experiences of African American women. The plays offer a critique of the dominant oppressive system under which black women are forced to suppress their wishes on the basis of hierarchical and patriarchal oppression. Her play, *Venus* is a mesmerizing and a terrifying tale of an African woman. The play shows that only an innately strong person could have survived for as long as Venus does. In spite of everything that happens to her, Venus refuses to be just a victim of oppression and exploitation. She resists as best as she can even in adverse circumstances. She accepts an offer made by Baron Doctor to move to France and display herself on stage after doing the same throughout the countryside. She takes it as an opportunity to earn money and secure herself economically. She cheerfully exclaims that she will receive 'Big bags of money!' Here Parks in a way empowers her central character. In her other play *In the Blood,* the protagonist Hester is both a victim and a killer. She is victimized owing to being a woman and her intense longing to be a good mother. Parks has depicted various aspects of African American experience. Through the protagonist, she tries to oppose the established hierarchical system of oppression of women by showcasing her resistance. Hester is an illiterate single mother with five children, each one of whom has a different father. Hester knows only the letter "A." Park depicts how her life experiences are informed by her race, class and gender. The combination of social, economic, physical, verbal and sexual violence pushes Hester towards the final eruption of long-contained rage and she batters her favourite son to death:

> Elam is correct in seeing Hester La Negrita's murder of Jabber as striking out against a social order that "not only restricts the roles of women and people of colour, but also preordains how one's offspring will function within this system. (qtd.in Kolin 101)

Jabber behaves like any other misogynist in Hester's life and treats his mother the way society had treated her throughout her life. Hester believes that five children whom she calls her treasure are actually her mistakes:

> Hester: Never shoulda had him.
>
> Never shoulda had none of em.
>
> Never was nothing but a pain to me:
>
> 5 Mistakes!. . . .
>
> I never shouldahaddem! (106-07)

Hansberry and Parks bring in intertextuality by depicting interconnectedness and rationality of the older texts and history. Intertextuality foregrounds the pattern of interconnectedness and interdependence between the new texts and the existing texts. Every text has some connections with the texts written earlier. "'The idea of the text, and thus of intertextuality, depends, as

Barthes argues, on the figure of the web, the weave, the garment (text) woven from the threads of the 'already written' and the already read" (qtd.in Allen 6). Whenever Parks borrows some subject, theme or storyline from any author's text, she focuses on using it as a base to build up the story instead of contradicting it or changing it altogether, so that one can see the glimpse of the old text again in the new text. Parks' works are separate from the old texts yet connected closely to them. They invite us to review the text from an entirely new stance by noticing the facts which we have perhaps missed out on or neglected in the first place. Her aim is to pass on the history and stories that are buried deep down. "[. . .] Parks' efforts cannot be reduced to mere mimicry; they are still wholly innovative. Each re-vision creates a next text, connects to, yet remains distinct from, the revised text" (Larson 4).

Her plays, *In the Blood* and *Fucking A* are based on Nathaniel Hawthorne's novel *The Scarlet Letter.* Hester in the play In *the Blood* and *Fucking A* is treated as an outcast just like the Hester of Nathaniel Hawthorne's *The Scarlet Letter.* Like Hester Prynne, Parks' Hester in *Fucking A*, also wears the Letter A above her left breast. This 'A' signifies the oppression, injustice and exploitation of black women who are branded as abortionists. Intertextuality, as Julia Kristeva has asserted, "has nothing to do with influence, sources, or even the stabilized model favoured in historical work of 'text' and 'context'. In this model, 'context' might explain 'text' but remains, ultimately, distinct from it" (qtd. in Allen 69). Lorraine Hansberry has also employed intertextuality in some of her plays. An interconnectedness of the text and context is visible in her play *A Raisin in the Sun* and the poem, "Harlem" by Langston Hughes. Both the texts explain the plight of Blacks. The questions that are posed in the poem related to Blacks' dreams are addressed by Hansberry as well in her play.

Cultural Memory plays a significant part in recreation of our past and history as it is connected with the African roots. As Simone Wells rightly says, "To be rooted is perhaps the most important and least recognised need of the Human soul" (qtd. in Rodriguez and Fortier7). It has the power to connect past, present and future, which helps newer generations to recall, remember, connect and explore history. While discussing cultural memory, we come across with the political, historical and economic struggle for survival of the marginalized. In their introduction to Memory & Cultural Politics, Amritjit Singh, Joseph Skerrett, Jr., and Robert Hogan discuss the African American "struggle to remember." They write:

> African American, brought hither in chains from their homes across the Atlantic, have struggled to remember a past from which they were cut off by the Middle Passage and slavery. As with Native Americans this feat of memory could not have been undertaken without conflict with the dominant national narrative, which denied any value to the African American past and its cultural products. (qtd. in Elam, Jr. and Kranser 9)

The black writers acknowledge that the historical and the cultural awareness became a vital tool for resistance as well as survival. In addition to the exquisite cultural memory, music continued to be a major form of African American dramatic writing. Music became the medium through which black writers depict the truth and emotions of Blacks' lives. Against a colonial backdrop, Hansberry and Parks strive to standardize African history through the use of explicit folkloric motifs and customs. They incorporate music which is a significant part of the blue aesthetic. Kalamu ya Salaam defines the blue aesthetic as:

> an ethos of blues people that manifests itself in everything done, not just music. As an African American literary motif, the Blues Aesthetic is grounded in the blues tradition and fortified by its connection to African American culture. In fact, the blues has become emblematic of the modern African American experience, giving a voice to the hardships of slavery, the challenges in adjusting to life beyond the plantation, of the Great Migration, of cultural immersion, and of finding a place and space within contemporary American society—all set against the backdrop of a guitar-laced melody. (qtd. in Washington 54)

Blues convey the sorrows and joy of Blacks' lives. Hansberry has stressed in all her plays that African heritage is integral for American men and women. She says, "the ultimate destiny and aspirations of the African people and twenty million American Negroes are inextricably and magnificently bound up together forever" (qtd. in Carter 36).

Based on several incidents of their childhood, Hansberry and Parks draw their themes from their personal experiences which give their plays an autobiographical touch. Their works are influenced by their personal lives and experiences. Both the writers have woven the essence of their experiences as black women. They mirror their actual plight and struggle. Although their plays are not solely autobiographical, both Hansberry and Parks take the origins of the themes of some of their plays from their childhood.

There are a few instances in *A Raisin in the Sun* that are taken directly from Hansberry's personal life. She addresses many of the issues that she had encountered in her life *in A Raisin in the Sun*, including racism, segregation, feminism, Africanism, and assimilation. The play depicts her life in a Chicago ghetto where she was born. "I think you could find the tempo of my people on their black porches. . . . Our Southside is a place apart: each piece of our living is a protest" (45). In 1937, her family moved into a home in the white Washington Park neighbourhood. The association wanted to enforce the race restrictive real estate covenant in place. The association members attempted to terrorise the Hansberry family during the court battle through violence. They confronted acute racism, and their home was attacked by a mob, with someone throwing a brick through the window. "Her father waged a legal battle to desegregate the white neighbourhoods and was victorious in the landmark Supreme Court case of Hansberry v. Lee, 311 U.S. 32" (Bloom 13). Hansberry's experience in Washington Park is thus central to *A Raisin in the Sun.*

Hansberry had a very strong respect for women in her life which is very much reflected in her play *A Raisin in the Sun.* Lena, the mother resembles her own mother, Nannie Perry Hansberry. Beneatha's character is Hansberry's own reflection. Her ideas reflect Lorraine Hansberry's ideology. Beneatha's tremendous efforts in striving for her goals are in a way reflection of Hansberry's own struggle as a young black woman playwright as she ponders:

> "May I?"
>
> And the voice of authority: "Yes you may –you may take one giant step."
>
> One drew in all one's breath and tightened one's fist and pulled the small body against the heavens, stretching,

> straining all the muscles in the legs to make — one giant step. (49)

To Be Young, Gifted and Black, an autobiographical play was adapted from Lorraine's own writing, letters, interviews, etc. It depicts her life from childhood to her illness, showcasing myriad aspects of her whole life and personality. "The play is the portrait of an individual, the workbook of an artist, and the chronicle of a rebel who celebrated the human spirit" (Nemiroff xviii). Though the play was adapted by Robert Nemiroff, Hansberry's husband, it was written in Hansberry's own words. In the play, Hansberry shares many of her memories. Remembering her mother, she says: "And I also remember my desperate and courageous mother, patrolling our house all night with a loaded German lugar, doggedly guarding her four children. . . ." (51).

Hansberry depicts how her parents asserted at the time of the birth registration of Hansberry and stated that they should be listed racially not as Negro but as Black. In part 1, Hansberry recalls her childhood when she was sent to kindergarten by her mother in white fur for which she was beaten up by the children there, assuming her to be a rich girl. She says that this incident made her a rebel. There are many such instances and memories from her life, which are reflected in the play.

Likewise, Parks also employs autobiographical elements in her plays. As Suzan-Lori Parks' father was in the army, she visited many places. That experience is reflected in her works. The fourth part of *Imperceptible Mutabilities in the Third kingdom*, reflects Parks' childhood, when her father used to stay away from the family for a long period due his posting in Army. Parks delineates the loss of identity and memory through the character, Sergeant Smith and his family – wife, two daughters and son. It is quite autobiographical as Parks' own family shares the same story. Parks' army officer father too, just like Sergeant Smith had to live far away from his wife, two daughters and a son as he was on duty:

> GARRETT: Might the fourth part of *Imperceptible Mutabilities* be a third cousin? There is another father who comes home from wars.
>
> PARKS: Those are some of the biggest memories I have of my father coming home from the war. (qtd. in Garret 186)

Parks said that *Father Comes Home from the Wars* reflects the time she spent in Texas with her family when her father was far away on duty in Vietnam. Thus, some of Parks' plays dramatize the return of the fathers after a long time depicting the consequent estrangement the family members experienced owing to a long separation from the head of the family and vice-versa. This represents the darker side of Parks' own personal experiences with her father. In an interview Parks accepts the presence of autobiographical element in her works:

> GARRETT: The weight of homecoming was a palpable presence in this performance.
>
> PARKS: Like I said, it's from my dad. My dad came home. From the Wars. . . . I'm just talking about something I know, something which I can really only emotionally understand by looking at it through a play, through the framework of the big picture. (qtd. in Garrett 189)

In *Imperceptible Mutabilities in the Third Kingdom*, Molly is bullied and excluded as she was not able to pronounce the words in the manner the white world demands. Parks relates it to one of her high school teachers who cautioned her not to be a writer because she could not spell words correctly, the way the white world demanded.

Though Lorraine Hansberry and Suzan-Lori Parks belong to different periods, differ in their literary techniques, they played a dominant role in the evolution of Black aesthetics in a powerful way. They turn the mirror towards Blacks, showing self-awareness, authentic representation of Blacks in contrast to the negative stereotypes perpetuated by the Whites. Both the playwrights endeavoured and succeeded in interrogating the authenticity of the history crafted by the Whites by relocating the actual identity of Blacks through their works.

The theme of assertion is incorporated in both the playwrights' works. Like Hansberry's characters, Parks' characters are victims of an oppressive society that denies them their identity and dignity. But these characters frequently express a desire to be heard and recognized. They express a desire for freedom. In Hansberry's *The Drinking Gourd,* Hannibal finally rebels against slavery in his own way. Similarly, in her other play, *Les Blancs*, Hansberry has depicted through the medium of the protagonist of the play, Tshembe, that violence is the only means left through which their voice can be heard. She further portrays the attitude of natives to revolt against the invaders who have disrupted their peaceful lives. In Parks' *The Death of the Last Black Man in the Whole Entire World*, the Black Man with Watermelon, is beaten and enslaved, but he always comes back to tell his story which is a way to retaliate. And another character from the play instructs him to write it down so that in future they'll know that they exist.

The major difference between these two writers is their style of writing. Lorraine Hansberry followed a naturalistic way of writing, interspersed with ideas and she used colloquial language in her plays. But Suzan-Lori Parks has a different style of writing. She rejected the naturalism of earlier drama and created a new type of theatre, one that has transcended conventions by radicalizing them. Her canon is quite experimental. She invented a new stage language where her characters speak an African American vernacular. "Emphasizing the Jazz roots, Parks has repeatedly described her plays in terms of "Rep & Rev," the repetition and revision of Jazz scores and themes. As she acknowledges, "Rep & Rev," is 'a central element in my work'" (Kolin 17). In her essay "Possession," Parks writes:

> Since history is a recorded or remembered event, theatre, for me, is the perfect place to 'make' history—that is, because so much of African- American history has been unrecorded, disremembered, washed out, one of my tasks as a playwright is to—through literature and the special strange relationship between theatre and real-life—locate the ancestral burial ground, dig for bones, find bones, hear bones sing, write it down. (4)

This book is a comparative study of the works of both the authors, Lorraine Hansberry and Suzan Lori Parks. It examines their works from the perspective of new historicism and post-colonialism, particularly in the context of racism and slavery, black feminism as well as the stylistic devices used by both. Comparing Hansberry and Parks, however, naturally brings out many similarities and some points of difference between the two. The book takes into account Lorraine Vivian Hansberry's *The Raisin in the Sun, The Drinking Gourd, Les Blancs, To Be Young, Gifted and Black* and Suzan-Lori Parks' *Imperceptible Mutabilities in the Third kingdom, Betting on the Dust Commander, The Death of the Last Man in the Whole Entire world, Pickling, The America Play, Venus, In the Blood, Fucking A, Topdog/ Underdog* and *Father Comes Home from the War.*

2
Being Black, Being Woman: Interrogating Dominant Paradigms

African American women writers have played an integral role in enriching African American literary tradition. Their writings address certain significant issues, which pertain not just to their predicament as black women but to black people as a whole. Black feminists aim at voicing the opinions of those who have been rendered silent and invisible in the prevailing patterns of society. Striving to demolish the social construction of black women's images and empower them by counteracting the falsified myths of negative black womanhood, Glenda Dickerson demonstrates that the traits of womanhood like beauty, femininity and morality are supposed to have been invested only in the white upper-class women who have been defined as chaste as opposed to black women who are depicted as unchaste and immoral. Black women have traditionally been categorized as ugly and masculine in Eurocentric discourses. Women across the globe are adversely affected by gender bias and are categorized as oppressed but African American women have been the victims of multiple forms of oppression. They are usually excluded from society on the pretext that they are incapable of any responsible work and should be relegated to subservient roles.

Black men and women had contributed equally for freedom during slavery but its only black men whose contribution is acknowledged. Consequently, they have been visible and have advanced in different spheres of life. Black women, on the other hand, have been offered only peripheral roles in society. Even after freedom from slavery, their lot did not improve much as their role was mainly confined to taking care of household needs and raising the children. Some black woman activists retaliated against such norms but many others submitted to their traditional roles. Moreover, black men had stood for eradicating racism but an end to sexism was never their concern. They remained ignorant to the dual victimization of black women on the basis of racist and sexist oppression.

African American women and white women see themselves differently in the contexts of race, class, and gender. White women's major concerns were to attain equal political, economic and educational rights, whereas black women were struggling for the survival. White women were not a racially suppressed group but African American women, whose lives were moulded by institutionalized racism, were inclined more severely to identify themselves as members of a racially marginalized group. White feminism has romanticized the black female experience instead of showing any concern for their dual victimization and oppression. bell hooks acknowledges their strength to manage or cope with their dual oppression solely, putting their sufferings completely in the background:

> Black women were told that we should find our dignity not in liberation from sexist oppression but in how well we could adjust, adapt, and cope. We had been asked to stand up and be congratulated for being "good little women" and then told to sit down and shut up. No one bothered to discuss the way in which sexism operates both independently of and simultaneously with racism to oppress us. (21)

Black women needed a movement that could exclusively address their problems and protect them from the sexism of black/white men and racism of white men/women. It was in the 1970s and 80s that what is called 'Black Women's Literary Renaissance', was fostered. They began to make their presence felt in political and social affairs. Way back in the sixties too, they had articulated their concerns but their voices remained largely unheard. Some African American women writers including Hansberry, Walker, Brooks among others had already gained visibility during these decades. But it was Toni Morrison's *The Bluest Eye* (1970) that foregrounded the devastating effect white ideals of beauty had on the young vulnerable black girls.As Audre Lorde puts it, "[W]riting is empowerment for others to speak out, step out and value their lives. It provides testimony of their experience as both individuals and members of community" (qtd. in Wisker 4). As black women's writing originates from black women's personal experiences in real life, it encapsulates their lives trapped in the imbroglio of racism and sexism as no male and white playwright could have done. The black feminist movement acknowledges the manifold oppression of black women at different levels. The exponents of the movement had realized that their problems cannot be overcome by focusing on a singular form of oppression and that issues like racism, classism and sexism need to be accosted together and at the same time. In 1973, National Black Feminist organization aimed at letting black women define themselves on their own. The stereotypical images of black womanhood perturbed them and hence they wanted to put forth the actual portrait of a black woman by reversing those images that had been passed down through history:

> The organization hoped to lend a strong political voice to the already established women's movement and to establish

> to the black liberation movement the need to acknowledge that only half the race could not be uplifted. (Beaulieu 69)

Black women knew that they were at the bottom of hierarchy but their understanding of race, class and gender was much better than their privileged counterparts. The following words of Zora Neal Hurston bear out the way black women have been treated as the mules of the world:

> Honey, de white man is the de ruler of everything as fur as Ah been able tuh find out. Maybe it's some place way off in de ocean where de black man is in power, but we don't know nothin' but what we see. So de white man throw down de load and tell de nigger man tuh pick it up. He picks it up because he have to, but he don't tote it. He hand it to his women folks. De nigger woman is de mule uh de world so fur as Ah can see. (qtd. in Collins 45)

Black women writers' oeuvre deals with deeply felt experiences of women—notions of beauty, economic insecurity, sexual abuse, love, relationships and above all search for an identity. Upholding her view specifically for African American women, bell hooks writes:

> To understand that finding a voice is an essential part of liberation struggle— for the oppressed, the exploited, a necessary starting place— a move in the direction of freedom, is important for those who stand in solidarity with us. (qtd. in Murphy 156)

Black feminist thought, hence, focuses on black women's empowerment and conditions of social justice. While exploring the common themes of a black women's standpoint, they tend to provide a distinct angle of vision where dominant groups have tried to suppress the black woman's consciousness and thoughts. Hannah Nelson notes, "I have grown to womanhood in a world where the saner you are, the madder you are made to appear" (qtd. in Collins 266). Black womanhood was trivialized for long and black women were regarded as co-conspirators rather than victims even when they were sexually exploited. Black women writers' consciousness was the outcome of their everyday and commonplace experiences. They finally succeeded in conveying the viewpoint that by rearticulating their resistance, they can be empowered. In the twentieth and twenty first centuries, African American women writers have mainly focused on the representation of black women as strong enough to face oppression and to overcome it. Contrary to the idea that black women become willing participants in their own oppression, their voices have dismantled these hegemonic assumptions. Most African American women do not accept the controlling images of theirs formed by Whites such as being mammies, mules, or sexually denigrated women. They have stood firm against all types of oppression.

A major theme in African American women writings is the theme of suffering and silencing of a woman, crushed down by 'the triple burden' of race, gender and class. The themes of motherhood, sisterhood, man-woman relationships, identity and women's roles are in some way or the other associated with this theme. Black women's writings showcase the challenging task of fighting for black liberation and gender equality simultaneously. Many of these women writers subsequently turned to the medium of theatre. Lynda Hart notes that theatre is the most effective of all literary genres for giving voice to the silenced voices:

> As a form, the drama is more public and social than other literary arts. The theatre is the sphere most removed from the confines of domesticity, thus the woman who ventures to be heard in the space takes greater risk than the woman poet or novelist, but it may also offer her greater potential effecting social change. (qtd. in Murphy 158)

Lorraine Hansberry and Suzan-Lori Parks emerged as powerful playwrights who uncompromisingly dealt with all aspects of the marginalization of black folk in general and black women in particular. Interlocking forms of race, gender, and class oppression have been an enduring theme in their works.

Their drama illuminates new and dark domains of specific experiences pertaining to the portrayal of negative images of the black female body and sexuality, silencing of black women's voice and the exclusion of black women from all the privileges given to Whites and men. Highlighting of these issues further led to an awakening against an unjust system. To quote Wiener, "Hansberry's writings anticipate the women's liberation movement that came to the forefront in America shortly after her death. She wrote a play that celebrated feminism before it had a name" (11). Margaret B. Wilkerson notes:

> With her statement, "I was born black and a female," Hansberry immediately established the "basis for tension" that informed her world view. Her consciousness of "ethnicity and gender . . . brought awareness of two key forces of conflict and oppression in the contemporary world. (236)

Mama in *A Raisin in the Sun* and Rissa in *The Drinking Gourd* exemplify Hansberry's concern with the idea of being black and being women perfectly. These are not just feminist issues. These issues bring to the surface the tension inherent in the very idea of life that these women lead. In an article titled "The Complex of Womanhood," Hansberry's most direct feminist statement, she draws attention to the realities underlying stereotypical images of a black woman:

> . . . On the one hand . . . she is saluted as a monument of endurance and fortitude, and in whose bosom all comforts reside . . . and, at the same time, another legend of the Negro woman describes the most . . . deprecating creature ever placed on earth to plague . . . the male. She is seen as an over-practical, unreasonable source of the destruction of all vision and totally lacking a sense of the proper "place" of womanhood. Either image taken alone is romance; put together they embrace some truths and present the complex of womanhood which . . . now awakens to find itself inextricably . . . bound to the world's most insurgent elements. . . . in the United States, a seamstress refuses one day, simply refuses, to move from her chosen place on a bus while an equally remarkable sister of hers ushers children past bayonets in Little Rock. It is indeed a single march, a unified destiny and the prize is the future. . . . On behalf of an ailing world which surely needs our defiance, may we, as Negroes or women never accept the notion of "our place." (qtd. in Friedman 77)

Hansberry's women suffer the onslaught of double jeopardy having seen many faces of oppression. In the structure of society Hansberry closely experienced, Whites ruled over Blacks, men ruled over women and subjects ruled over what were seen as objects. With this kind of domination, black women were at the lowest rung in this entire system of oppression. They were relegated to their 'natural' inferior role, an idealized vision of women in home where they were treated brutally by black men. The conventional theatre has propagated patriarchal ideology which advocates hierarchical ordering of gender-based differences in order to serve the interests of men. The female world has long been dominated by the patriarchal powers which hold legitimacy over them. Silencing any attempts to articulate this oppression was the worst form of tyranny.

Hansberry's and Parks' major objective is to retrieve black womanhood from oblivion to recognition. They disrupt the stereotypical prejudices, cultural conventions and gender-based constraints that had been created by white/ male dominated world. These playwrights give voice to the voiceless in order to make them heard all around the world. By doing so they enrich the understanding of the African American culture and black women's struggle against politics of race, gender and class which undermine their existence and identity. They crash landed on the American stage with new images of resilient and powerful black women, images which were not limiting in any way. They replaced the notion of black women as frigid, immoral, promiscuous and helpless by portraying them as heroic and strong, capable of resisting servitude and racial denigration that had conditioned them for ages.

Hansberry's acknowledgement of being black and a female was the starting point for her philosophical journey from Chicago to the world community. Hence, it was this empathy that facilitated a poignant delineation of the plight of black women in *A Raisin in the Sun*. Her portrayal of Beneatha and Ruth represents this plight. Hansberry observed an interview with the well-known social historian Studs Terkel in 1959, "Obviously the most oppressed group of any oppressed group will be its women, who are twice oppressed" (qtd. in Wiener 11). This double oppression is reflected in *A Raisin in the Sun* through the three women characters in the play, Lena Younger, Ruth and Beneatha. Vastly different from one another, they are courageous and revolutionary women who struggle for the betterment of their family. Mama has lost her husband; still she tries her level best to keep her family united. She works for long hours for a wealthy white family. Ruth works as a domestic help for white families and thinks to abort her baby for her family's better future. Beneatha bravely resists sexism of her conservative boyfriend, her African mentor and her own selfish and dominating brother. Hansberry was ahead of her times in her attitude towards masculinity and femininity. As bell hooks writes, "Looking at the world from a standpoint that recognized the interconnectedness of race, sex, and class, she challenged everyone who encountered her work" (qtd. in Wiener 12-13). This is clear from the portrayal of the character of Ruth, wife of Walter Lee. She faces racism as she has to work for a white family. Secondly, she is dominated by her husband. And thirdly, she suffers because of her poverty. Hansberry presents the black domestic who must clean the kitchens of white women as well as her own. At the same time, she is expected to bolster the male ego which has been deflated by racism and poverty. She has to take care of her children, her family but still she never gets the respect and position she is worthy of. She remains in a highly vulnerable position all her life and is constantly pushed to the brink. Remaining invisible in family and society, she is expected to be a doormat. The play underpins the tragic predicament of a black woman and emphasizes that black women in contrast to white women suffer much more.

Black Activist Anna Julia Cooper sums up the African American woman's position in these words: "She is confronted by a woman question and a race problem, and is as yet an unknown or unacknowledged factor in both" (qtd. in James 14). Margaret B. Wilkerson has called her "the complete Feminist, for she sought to address both race and gender within a social context" (qtd. in Beaulieu 392). In *A Raisin in the Sun,* Hansberry refers to both these unacknowledged factors vis-à-vis the characters she creates. Hansberry's own statement about being black and a woman finds a perfect echo in Cooper's observation. *A Raisin in the Sun* is a powerful play that interrogates dominant paradigms proving that alternative voices and voices of dissent cannot be stifled forever. The play is essentially a portrait of black family in America that predated the explosive revolution in black and feminist movement. It anticipates the transformation in gender relations in America. Though each of the women in the play, Mama, Ruth and Beneatha represent different generations and experiences, throughout the play they are seen furthering their roles as women whereas Walter Lee, the male character attempts to prove his worth by belittling the women in his life. Walter Lee holds conventional views on gender, and links his own identity and self-worth to his sense of manhood:

> Walter represents a broken masculinity, specifically pertaining to African-American men of the 1950s who were shut out of the American Dream by racism and economic oppression. Because of this exclusion, Walter's dreams of success and money become tied to his perceptions of himself and his manhood. (Bloom 33)

Issues of masculinity and femininity are deeply woven in this play presenting a microcosm of society. In traditional societies, the male member of the family is considered as a dominant force and the only strength of the family. The relationship between Walter and Beneatha, as brother and sister and the relationship between Walter and Ruth, as husband and wife depict the construct of male superiority that has governed the world. Women are shown as inferior to men in all aspects. The streak of patriarchal dominance is visible throughout the play through different male characters. In the very beginning of the play, in act 1, scene 1, Walter says to his wife Ruth:

> WALTER: First thing a man ought to learn in life is not to make love to no colored woman first thing in the morning. You all some eeevil people at eight o'clock in the morning. (27)

He adds:

> That is just what is wrong with the colored women in this world . . . Don't understand about building their men up and making 'em feel like they somebody. Like they can do something. (34)

Walter wants that woman in his life should unconditionally support him, obey him and make him feel like a man who has absolute freedom to live life his own way and to act according to his own judgment. He considers Ruth's strength as a threat to his manhood but Hansberry straightaway rejects the emasculating black women stereotype by depicting the real causes of frustration which include the race prejudice and economic oppression which affect black men and women alike.

According to Walter, men are naturally inclined to dominate women as social division places black women in a very low position. Walter comments that black women are the world's most backward race of the people. He keeps on making blanket statements on black women and believes that women's profound influence on family decisions is an assault on his manhood. He considers women's strength as his weakness. Ruth is always subordinate to him. Walter is a very domineering husband and he invariably rubbishes her decisions as he is of the opinion that a woman has no right to decide anything on her own. When Ruth refuses to give money to Travis, Walter scolds her and fulfils Travis's demand by giving him money against his wife's wishes. Walter reprimands Ruth for giving Travis an impression that they cannot afford fifty cents. Walter not only gives Travis the fifty cents that he has requested, but he also gives him extra fifty cents. In doing so Walter tries to change his image in his son's eyes and asserts his manhood at the same time. In his struggle to reclaim his masculinity, he makes racist and sexist comments to Ruth, "We one group of men tied to a race of women with small mind! (35) While discussing sexism among blacks in her essay, *In Search of Our Mothers' Garden*, Alice Walker writes:

> I tell her how important I feel this is: that black men not take out their anger and frustration on their . . . Coretta's face is thoughtful as she says, "Maybe I . . . I have but few black men seem to feel secure enough as men that they can make women feel like women. (151-52)

Walter's attitude towards his sister Beneatha is also the same. When she shares her dream to be a doctor with her brother, Walter Lee, instead of appreciating and supporting her, questions her commitment to become a doctor and says disheartening things about black women. Walter suggests that she should change her mind as she does not need to be a doctor but only a nurse or someone's wife like any other woman:

> WALTER: Who the hell told you had to be a doctor? If you so crazy 'bout messing 'round with sick people—then go be a nurse like other women—or just get married and be quite. . . . (38)

Walter discourages Beneatha by commenting that women are fit only for supporting roles. And like Walter, both of Beneatha's suitors display male chauvinism. For George Murchison, Beneatha's dream and desire to be a doctor is funny and laughable. He considers Beneatha beautiful but not intelligent and expects her to remain silent most of the time. He is never interested in discussing serious matters with Beneatha. He never tries to understand her feelings. When she tries to engage with him seriously, he advises her:

> GEORGE:. . . . The moody stuff . . . I don't like it. You're a nice-looking girl . . . That's all you need, honey, forget the atmosphere. Guys aren't going to go for the atmosphere –they're going to go for what they see. Be glad for that. Drop the Garbo routine. It doesn't go with you. As for myself, I want a nice —simple –sophisticated girl . . . not a poet–O.K.? (96)

The statement implies George's superficiality and his attitude towards women. He believes a woman is not capable of doing anything great in her life and deserves to be discouraged if she is ambitious. He believes that ambition in women is equal to a sin.

Beneatha's other suitor, Joseph Asagai, though presented in a more favourable light than George, is also sexist. In act 1, scene 2, Asagai mocks the notion of a "liberated" woman when Beneatha expresses her view to have a career for herself. He says,

"It is how you can be sure that the world's most liberated women are not liberated at all. You all talk about it too much" (64).

Thus, Hansberry poignantly defines the complexities and social tensions that black women face. While addressing the male/female dichotomy through relationships between brother and sister, husband and wife, son and mother in the play, Hansberry traces the struggles and conflicts within an African American family.

Suzan-Lori Parks also showcases the society shaped by the bondage of racism, sexism and classism where black woman suffers the most in this intersecting system of power. Her play, *In the Blood* is based on Nathaniel Hawthorne's *The Scarlet Letter* which depicts the saga of Hester, who commits adultery in a puritan society. The protagonist is treated as an outcast by being forced to bear the mark of the letter 'A' for her act of indulging in adultery. Similarly in Parks' play *In the Blood*, the central character who shares the same name, Hester, is depicted as an outcast because she gives birth to five children out of wedlock. Hester is a homeless mother who lives under a bridge and strives hard in life in order to raise her children. Each child has a different father but she doesn't get help from any. She is also marked by the letter 'A' as this is the only English alphabet she knows. The play begins with a prologue in which the chorus mocks her as being an illiterate woman who "CANT READ CANT WRITE". In addition, they all refer to her as a 'SLUT,' a 'HUSSY' and a 'BURDEN TO SOCIETY':

> THATS WHY THINGS ARE BAD LIKE THEY ARE
>
> CAUSE OF

GIRLS LIKE THAT. . . .

SHE GOT FIVE OF THEM

FIVE BRATS

AND NOT ONE OF THEM GOT A DADDY. (5)

Parks slams the hypocrisy of society where there are separate parameters to assess men and women. *In the Blood* is a realistic play, where she poses a question on the traditional construct of femininity. Hester is an outcast, a socially unfit being and hence to be communally excluded from the so-called sophisticated society. Through Hester, Parks depicts how the character of a black woman is misrepresented. Her image is tainted by the stain of being a mother of five children from five different fathers without getting married. Nobody has ever raised any question on those fathers who have abandoned her and their children but Hester is treated as an outcast throughout the play.

Parks powerfully highlights the social oppression of black women owing to discrimination, violence, sexual harassment and domination that they face. Since colonial era, there have been racially created gendered images of African American women. They had been stigmatized with the reputation of being lascivious and unchaste. Though the African American women were forcefully compelled to have sexual relationships with their masters, the blame was always placed on them and they were labelled sluts.

In the first scene of *In the Blood*, Hester, being illiterate, is seen asking her son Jabber the meaning of the word 'SLUT' which has been written on their wall. She wants to learn the word because she believes that by educating herself, she will be able to overcome the oppression she is facing. Jabber refuses to do so as he doesn't want to hurt his mother's feelings. She asks him, "Zit uh good word or a bad word?" (9). Though at the end of the play, Jabber finally reads it and repeats it again and again which leads to his murder by his own mother as she finds the word an assault on her dignity. Jabber eventually behaves like any other misogynist in Hester's life. By murdering her son, Hester stands against the white/male domineering world which has branded her in a negative manner. Throughout the dramatic narrative, Hester is exploited and used by many. Chilli and Reverend D humiliate her, the fathers of two of her children (Jabber and Baby, respectively), they refuse to own up their role in violating her. Similarly, the white women, The Welfare Lady, the Doctor, the embodiment of the Medicare system; and Amiga Gringa, her homeless 'white' friend, show no kindness towards her. All of them consider Hester inferior to them in all aspects which results in triple marginalization of Hester. Instead of providing any assistance to Hester, they end up being responsible for her sad plight. However, together they believe that Hester is the architect of her own ruin. Single motherhood, destitution and a life of disrespect seem to them as things she was instrumental in choosing for herself.

Through the medium of confession by each culpable figure in Hester's life, Parks brings to the fore their disgusting attitudes. The Doctor treats Hester in an inhuman manner as if she is an animal. Parks describes him carrying all of his office paraphernalia on his back. He begins to examine her in public as she has stomach pain due to the lack of regular meals:

> Doctor: Howreyr meals?
>
> Hester: The kids come first.

Doctor: Course they do. Howreyr bowels. Regular?

Hester: I dunno. . . .

Doctor: In a minute. Gimmie the Spread & Squat right quick. Lets have a look under the hood. (39)

According to the Doctor the best possible way for Hester to get rid of all her problems and tensions is to have herself sterilized. He recommends her to remove her woman parts in order not to beget more children. His sick mentality is reflected in the way he advises her to be usurped of her womanhood, motherhood, and femininity forever. Besides, he uses Hester's body to satisfy his lust but blames her to be the one who is responsible for this. He portrays himself as a helpless victim. In his confession, he declares:

Doctor: I was

lonesome and

she gave herself to me in a way that I had never experienced

even with women I've paid

she was, like she was giving me something that was not

hers to give me

but something that was mine

that I'd lent her

and she was returning it to me. . . .

What could I do?

I couldn't help it. (44)

And later he pretends as if he is a man of compassion who cares for the suffering humanity. He justifies having exploited

Hester by highlighting the class difference, as though that provided him the license to violate a woman of the lower class, whom he could not have living with him:

> Doctor: Times are tough:
>
> What can we do?
>
> When I see a woman begging on the streets I guess
>
> I could bring her in my house . . . .
>
> make her a member of my family, sure.
>
> But there are hundreds and thousands of them
>
> and my house can't hold them all. . . .
>
> They wouldn't really fit in with us.
>
> There is such a gulf between us. What can we do? (44)

The welfare lady's confession also puts emphasis on the issue of class divide. She herself is Black but thinks herself to be of a superior kind. She and the Doctor exploit Hester for sexual purposes. Welfare confesses that she and her husband had a "threesome" with Hester to add something new to their sexual life. The deep-seated prejudice against what is described as the hyper-sexuality of an African American women is brought to the fore here. In her confession, the Welfare Lady says:

> Welfare Lady: And I should emphasize that she is a low-class person. What I mean by that is that we have absolutely nothing in common. As her caseworker I realize that maintenance of the system depends on a well-drawn boundary line and all parties respecting that boundary. And I am, after all, I am a married woman. (62)

Hence, Hester is victimized by her own black people too, who pretend to help her but just contribute towards her exploitation. Likewise other characters, namely Reverend D' who himself is black and Chilli, both the fathers of her two children are equally responsible for Hester's social oppression as they neither accept her nor her children. To add to her misery, they do not even support her financially. In scene 7, Chilli, the father of the elder son, Jabber comes back and tells Hester his wish to marry her but he shows male dominance by saying that he has some conditions to which Hester has to agree. He brings props like veil, dress and a ring which symbolize femininity. He compares her with Virgin Mary and says:

> Chilli: I carry around this picture of you. Sad and lonely with our child on yr hip. Struggling to make do. Struggling against all odds. And triumphant. Triumphant against everything. Like—hell, like Jesus and Mary. And if they can do it so could my Hester. My dear Hester. Or so. I thought. But I don't think so. (96)

He discards her when he meets all of her children from different fathers. Hester keeps on pleading but Chilli is arrogant as ever and rejects her indignantly. Reverend D', father of her other child also finds it degrading and embarrassing to even accept that he and Hester had some relationship with each other. These instances reflect the hypocrisy of a male-dominated society. Amiga Gringa and Hester are from the same class and have suffered patriarchal oppression alike but Amiga acts superior to Hester because of her race. She claims that her white womb makes her more valuable as people desire children from her whereas Hester's black womb is worthless. Her patronizing attitude and false superiority are clearly reflected in their conversation when Hester assures her of getting some sewing work for her:

> Hester: I bet I could get you some sewing.
>
> Amiga Gringa: Oh no. That's not for me. If I work, Hester, I would want to be paid a living wage. You have agreed to work for less than a living wage. May as well be a slave. Or an animal.
>
> Hester: It's a start. She said if I do well—
>
> Amiga Gringa: If you do well she's gonna let you be her slave for life. Wouldn't catch me doing that. Chump work. No nono. But it's a good thing you are. Examples to the Kids. (66)

The most significant fact that comes out of these confessions is that all the characters totally refuse to take any kind of responsibility for Hester's plight. Parks deals with specific questions of black women's experience by identifying black female subject particularly in terms of male/female relationship. In her play *Betting in the Dust Commander*, Parks depicts the relationship between two characters, Lucius who is a dominating husband and his wife Mare, a self-sacrificing and submissive person. As Jacqueline Wood observes:

> The name Mare, as Lucius calls his wife, while an obvious derivation of Mary . . . is certainly reminiscent of ZoraNeale Hurston's representation that the black woman is 'de mule uh de world,' carrying implications of breeder, beast of burden, commodity. (37)

Lucius' conduct throughout the play reveals his dissatisfaction with his marriage which he thinks is not as good as he assumed it would be. Though he pretends that he cares for Mare's stuck eyes and hung cries but actually he doesn't care at all. Both of them are shown struggling with the complexities and tensions of married life. They repeatedly discuss about replacing fresh flowers with the plastic ones which not only shows their wish to retain their memories but also Lucius' revulsion for real flowers/reality and the actual obligations of being married. Mare's dealing with her domineering partner can be compared to a bird yearning to be free. She exclaims, "Shouldn't put no animal in plastic. Animal should breathe free" (80). These lines reflect Mare's own suffocation in an oppressive marriage. She feels stifled in her relationship with Lucius as he always criticizes and threatens to leave her. She dreams of a bird's life by seeing it breathe only to invite Lucius ridicule.

Alice Walker in her essay, *In Search of Our Mothers' Garden*, refers to the African American women's suppressed talent, and artistic skills, which gave them succour in the vicious cycle of slavery and subjugation. She imagines "writing back through our mothers," to use Tegan Zimmerman's phrase and tries to evoke the silenced African American women whose creativity is buried under the yoke of oppression. She further adds:

> Yet so many of the stories that I write, that we all write, are my mother's stories . . . through years of listening to my mother's stories of her life, I have absorbed not only the stories themselves, but something of . . . the urgency that involves the knowledge that her stories—like her—must be recorded. (qtd. in Murphy 157)

She also refers to the story of Phillis to point out the fact that African American women were not given the opportunity to exploit their capabilities. Beneatha too is similar to Phillis as there are so many hurdles in her life too which prevent her from achieving her goals. Her talent and her enthusiasm to do something in life are constantly suppressed by the male members who live around her.

In her play *Pickling*, Parks idealizes the past and roles of women in those times through her only character, Miss Miss in the play. Miss Miss is an agoraphobic old maid who is stricken with a sense of alienation and sees herself as an isolated black female. She addresses herself in third person "Miss Miss." She is devoid of any identity in the outside world as she is always confined to her house, ". . . good I've got everythin I need right here at my fingertips never need to go outside is over-whelming sstoo much. Havent been out since. Synce uh comedinlass. Hee! Got it all here" (94). It seems that her voice is trapped inside the house which suggests her fear to face the outside world. The portrait of Miss Miss depicts the predicament of a caged black woman, whose life is a saga of pain and suffering. Though she longs for the company of her lover Charles, her brave life-guard whom she also calls "Professional savior", she suspects that Charles comes not to see her but to eat the pickled beets which she had prepared with the help of her mother when she was alive. She feels that Charles has betrayed her and broken her trust by not only destroying her cupboard but also her body. Thus, Parks depicts the catastrophic upshot of dependent relationships on black women. As Collins said, "Black women are confronted with the challenge of interlocking structures of race, class, and gender oppression while rejecting and transcending those same structures" (qtd. in Wood 40). Thus, *Betting on the Dust Commander* and *Pickling* deal with the plight of black women and raise specific questions on black women's existence and identity where they face loss of female selfhood.

Black Women's Bodies: Objectifying the 'Other'

Annals of slavery reveal that a black woman's body was historically showcased as an object for consumption. Colonialism served as the basis for sexualization and racialization of black women's bodies. To reinforce the notion of white superiority, the bodies of black women were used not just for sexual services but also subjected to hard labour so as to ensure comfortable life full of leisure for white men as well as white women. Myriad images of African American women, being sexually denigrated have been formed in order to justify gender, race and class oppression by the Whites. The portrayal of black women as animalistic and lustful is a justification of the abuse of black women. Delia Jarrett-Macauley in her book *Reconstructing Womanhood, Reconstructing Feminism: Writings on Black Women* quotes a thirty- two year old black woman Housing Officer:

> It is "white" men who see the Black woman as an unsatisfied mamma just to be used sexually . . . Black women are seen as sexual animals. For example, in the media they are beasts. The Black woman is an unsatiated mamma who can satisfy you. You are just to be used any way and not to be seen as a person. As a human being you are used and thrown away like rubbish. (qtd. in Marshall13)

In colonial era, it was considered a matter of right and privilege of the white master to watch and abuse a black body:

> The notion that woman is constructed as living gift or donation of herself to the fulfilment of all others' desires and needs— i.e., to making everyone else happy—is an originary myth that is still in need of deconstruction. . . .

> How are Black women's bodies seen and repressed under the Western, male, patriarchal "gaze"? (qtd. in Davies 20)

Similar conception is demonstrated by Parks in her plays *Venus* and *Imperceptible Mutabilities in the Third Kingdom*. *Venus* is embellished with historical and fictional details which highlight the disregard and mistreatment of black women, their bodies and their mind. In the play, the act of watching plays a vital role in identity (de)formation. Venus becomes the object of lust and curiosity of Whites. Mother-showman, her caretaker, asks her to undress and present herself naked for the gluttonous white spectators. Likewise in *Imperceptible Mutabilities in the Third Kingdom*, in "Snails" white naturalist contrives a large roach in the room to spy on three black girls as if they were animals or insects. He tries to observe their behaviour and tells his students that they must watch the subjects when they believe that nobody can see them.

Black women's body is portrayed as a mechanized, dehumanized and animalized slave body which is an embodiment of sexual promiscuity. This image promoted the representation of Saartjie Baartman (Sarah Bartmann), the so-called Hottentot Venus, whose body was showcased for the pleasure of European spectators. Venus symbolizes the indignity foisted upon African American women in the colonial era. In *Venus,* the protagonist represents all the black women who are disregarded, humiliated and brutalized throughout their lives under white supremacy and patriarchal domination. Suzan-Lori Parks juxtaposes the historical and fictional details that chronicle the mistreatment and discomfiture in black women's lives. It unfolds the saga of a black woman's yearning and longing for love. It depicts how a black woman struggles in a hostile and unfeeling world. Parks tries to re-create the true story of Saartjie Baartman and exposes the most detestable saga of racism, objectification and oppression. The real Saartjie was given the name Hottentot Venus (the name Parks also uses in the play). She was brought from Africa to Europe during the colonial period. Her nude body with her large hips was unabashedly put on public display for the white Europeans in London and Paris during the early nineteenth century. She died in Paris in 1815 at the age of 26. Even after her death, her body continued to be exposed for scientific reasons. Her corpse was dissected by the French naturalist Georges Cuvier who is named as the Baron Docteur in the play. Her genitalia were preserved and displayed at the Musee de l' Homme in Paris. Parks uses history in her play but does not solely develop the play on the objectification of the black woman's body. In fact, she invests Venus with power to resist as a black woman who uses her situation and circumstances as an opportunity to grow as best as possible from a victim to an assailant.

In the play, Venus is also exposed to the public view. The Brother and The Man convince The Girl (Venus) to go with them to England where they will present her and her large buttocks as a freak show attraction. The prejudices that existed against black women's bodies are borne out by the following observation:

> During the nineteenth century it was claimed that the inherent abnormality and pathology of Black female genitalia signified that Blacks were a separate and lower race. Thereby the genitalia of the Black woman indicated that she was diseased, bestial and unapproachable. The contradictory sexualized figure of Blacks was linked to genitalia that were defined as complete yet damaged,

> diseased yet attractive, poisoning yet potent. Consequently, Black female genitalia represented sexual pathology, corruption and death. (Marshall 8)

Objectification is central to the subordination of black women and relegates them to the lowest rung of society. The black woman is categorized as the 'Other' who is viewed as an object to be controlled and exploited. Parks depicts the sexual objectification and exploitation of black women in her play *Venus*. The vulnerability of Venus is highlighted when she is reduced to an object who is exploited by the Whites for their personal gains. Mother Showman expresses her view that the English like that sort of thing and that's how they would cash in on this. Venus knows that the scientist is fascinated by her. She is naïve and cherishes the illusion that the scientist loves her and hence establishes a sexual relationship with him. She is, however, eventually abandoned by him. After her death, he dissects her body. In an interview Parks justifies Venus's decision to go with the Doctor. She says:

> Venus wants to go with the man who has clean hands and who is nice, instead of staying with the Mother Showman who beats her and steals from her and invites men to rape her. . . . Her dream of a better life, is so beautiful and she just misses realizing it. She misses realizing her dream to be someone of means who could send money home and maybe go home and live as a wealthy woman. (qtd. in Wetmore, Jr 137-38)

Colonialism led to black women being stereotyped as negative, sensuous, bestial, and hypersexual so as to justify their exploitation. "As Black women were relegated to the category of sensuous slaves . . . this provided a forceful legitimation for their sexual abuse by 'white' men" (Marshall 6). Parks portrays Baron Docteur as a person who treats Venus as an object rather than as a beloved. He takes measurements of her living body. Later in scene 7, titled She'll Make a Splendid Corpse, when Baron Docteur comes to know that Venus is pregnant, he gets worried because he doesn't want to accept her in public. He says, "God. Is there anything we can do about it? I've a wife. A career. A reputation. Is there anything we can do about it we together in privacy of my office" (130). Later in Scene 7, With The Chorus of Anatomists, it is mentioned that the measurements of Venus' limb-bones will of course be corrected after maceration, which is a process performed after death, when body parts are soaked in a chemical solution to separate the flesh from the bones. Parks' play underscores Venus' vulnerability and naivete who asks Baron Docteur the meaning of maceration:

> THE VENUS: Whats "maceration." . . . .
>
> THE BARON DOCTEUR: Whyd you ask?
>
> THE VENUS: They always say:
>
> "themeasurementsll be corrected after
>
> maceration." What it mean?
>
> THE BARON DOCTEUR: "Macerations" French for "lunch". . . . (141)

The Docteur comes out with the hypothesis after dissecting Venus' body, that Blacks are essentially inferior to Whites. Thus, he humiliates and commodifies black female body. Venus' brain is compared to white woman's brain to highlight the fact that black women are less intelligent than Whites. And her autopsy leads anatomists and spectators to focus on her sexual organs. The similar viewpoint about black women is reflected through the lines of court ruling as well which highlights the discrimination between Europeans and Africans:

> THE CHORUS OF THE COURT
>
> It is clear shes got grand plots and plans
>
> to make her mark and her mint by playing outside the bounds so that we find
>
> Her person much depraved but she sez her show is part of Gods great plan and we buy that .
>
> Besides she has the right to make her mark just like the Dancing Irish Dwarf. . . .
>
> it is very much to the credit of our great country
>
> that even female Hottentot can find a court to review her
>
> status. (84)

The court ruling also suggests and tries to justify the hierarchy based on racial prejudice in the name of great plan of God. Mother Showman also considers Venus as "The very lowest rung on Our Lords Great Evolutionary Ladder! She boastfully says that she kicks her like a dog" (55).

Baron Docteur represents the embodiment of white desire. He gives Venus the disease of Chlamydia and when he comes to know that she could probably die, he abandons her and imprisons her to hasten her death. He wants to dissect her and own some fame out of it as a great scientist at the cost of her exploitation. At the end Venus requests Docteur to kiss her and says, "*Kiss* me *Kiss* me *Kiss* me *Kiss*" which reflects her yearning to be accepted and recognized by the person whom she had loved. But her lover,

Baron Docteur who is the representative of the white world, doesn't pay much heed to her deep feelings and ends up only exploiting her:

> THE BARON DOCTEUR: Ive got wife. You've got a homeland and a family back there.
>
> THE VENUS: I don't wanna go back inny more.
>
> I like yr company too much.
>
> Besides, it was a shitty life. (109)

This perception ultimately leads to fostering black women's oppression. In *Fucking A* and *Venus*, the black women are sexually exploited by white men who were already married and never accept these women as their own in public. When Canary in *Fucking A*, asks Mayor to marry her as promised, Mayor replies:

> Mayor: They will demand that I remarry a woman of a— of a certain background. My heart will be split in two . . . I am their humble civil servant. cannot let them down . . . . But nothing between us will change.
>
> Canary: You said youd marry me.
>
> You gave your word. I love you.
>
> Mayor: I have the future of my country to consider
>
> . . . .
>
> "Wife," "Mistress," what does it matter?
>
> Take gold. Buy something nice. (153)

Canary and Venus don't have control over their own bodies. Mayor in *Fucking A* and Docteur in *Venus* abuse black women but do not love them. Both the women finally make a choice in order to use white men for financial and social gain. Even as Suzan- Lori Parks emphasizes that poverty necessitates their submission, the fact remains that the oppressed were actually never given a choice. This is the reason why Black feminist view looks for deconstructing sexualized identities of black women created by European colonizers. They strive to obliterate the estrangement between black women's identity and the way her image is stereotyped in society justifying her subordination by Blacks and Whites. Patricia Hill Collins asserts, "the controlling images applied to Black women are so uniformly negative that they almost necessitate resistance if black women are to have any positive self-images" (qtd. in Marshall 30).

African American women playwrights defy these stereotypical portrayals of black women by subverting the Eurocentric notions by depicting the real and the actual side of black women's experiences. They portray black women's authentic reality. By presenting the protagonists of her plays, *In the Blood, Fucking A* and *Venus* as victims of sexual harassment, Suzan-Lori Parks succeeds in contradicting black women's controlling image which mystifies them as temptresses who employ their sexual urges in order to attract and trap white men.

The Jezebel stereotype was consistently utilized by the white masters in order to justify their atrocities against black women. According to the Jezebel myth, the black women were seen as sexually active females who would entice white men to satisfy their sexual fantasies. This idea is further driven home by Lorraine Hansberry who creates three characters in her autobiographical play, *To Be Young, Gifted and Black*: a young domestic worker; a chic, professional, middle-aged woman; and a mother in her thirties. Each speaks a variant of the same idea:

> In these streets out there, any little white boy from Long Island or Westchester sees me and leans out of his car and yells— "Hey there, *hot chocolate!* Say there, Jezebel! Hey you— 'Hundred Dollar Misunderstanding'! YOU! Bet you know where there's a good time tonight . . ." Follow me sometimes and see if I lie. I can be coming from eight hours on an assembly line or fourteen hours in Mrs. Halsey's kitchen. I can be all filled up that day with three hundred years of rage so that my eyes are flashing and my flesh is trembling—and the white boys in the streets, they look at me and think of sex. They look at me and that's all they think. . . . Baby, you could be Jesus in drag—but if you're brown they're sure you' reselling! (98)

Parks' play *Fucking A*, is a feminist play which outlines issues like rape, pregnancy, motherhood, abortion and sexuality. It depicts patriarchal society in which men have an upper hand, taking major decisions and having a full control on women's body. The play shows that a woman who cannot give birth to a child is accorded a lower status compared to the woman who can be a mother. Nobody ever questions a man. In scene 2, The Mayor calls his wife's infertility "disgraceful" and a national disgrace. He says, "Yr a disgrace to the nation. Everyone agrees. I should remove you from our townhouse and put you in a country house" (129). However, when Mayor finds that she is pregnant, he changes his mind. Hence, the life of his wife is dictated by his whims and fancies. Mayor also insists upon the importance of the gender of the child when he says, "And those people elected me to lead for the rest of my life and when they elected me they expected me to produce a son . . . that son to lead for the rest of his life and so on and so on and so on" (127). He adds, "They look up to me and they see my right hand dangling. Where I should be holding the hand of my son or perhaps have my arm resting proudly on the young man's shoulder . . . but my right hand is dangling empty, Woman" (128).

Thus, Mayor's claim that people had elected him and they expect that his son should lead afterwards reflects the mindset of a majority of people according to which a higher position can only be transferred to a male and a White. Under the pretext of benefiting the society, he is fulfilling his own personal desires.

Also, Parks' plays *In the Blood* and *Fucking A* are the narratives of mothers who are compelled to kill their own children owing to the adverse living conditions of the African American women, usually at the bottom of the social scale. Hester is forced to have surgery to remove away her "woman's parts." The African American woman has no control over her body. The black body is a site where violence and oppression are manifested consistently. Parks' *In the Blood* criticizes the objectification of African American female body which is used just to gratify others' sexual desires. In one of his visits to Hester, Doctor announces that Hester will have to have a hysterectomy, referenced as a 'removal of your womanly parts', because of the number of children she has had— each by a different father. His state-sponsored intervention suggests that Hester doesn't practice safe-sex which consequently leads to unwanted births of children creating problems for society. As a result, she, like an animal, must be corrected— 'fixed'.

Parks deals with the theme of exploitation of African American women in her play *Imperceptible Mutabilities in the Third Kingdom*. In part 1, "Snails" of the play the three young black women are spied on as subjects by a white scientist, Dr. Lutzky, who later submits a report of his experimentation on three women whom he calls "roaches" or "Primitives". He claims that they need help to survive in this modern world. Molly objectifies herself, as she recollects the memories of black people on the Middle Passage, who were threatened to be "jettisoned" and were actually jettisoned from the ship. The African American girls know the necessity of articulating their stories but they fail to do so because they are trapped in circumstances beyond their control.

Quest for identity

Black feminists have frequently pondered over the issues related to embodiment, dignity and identity of the black woman. From the epoch of enslavement, black women have been perpetually struggling for equality. Racism and sexism have further complicated the struggle of a black woman for identity. The question of identity in feminist theory is central and throws light on the understanding the female subjectivity and gender construction by illustrating it through the experience of black women. It talks about the visibility/ invisibility of black women in society.

Black women's right to define themselves is taken away from them by objectifying them. Treating Black women as animals and not human beings is in itself a form of objectification. bell hooks rightly asserts, "As objects, one's reality is defined by others, one's identity created by others, one's history named only in ways that define one's relationship to those who are subject" (qtd. in Collins 71). Black women writers have emphasized on the interconnectedness of race, gender, class, education, work, and sexuality in constructing black women's identities. Thus, identity emerges as a major issue in black women's writings which specifically focus on their rights to construct their own identities.

Lorraine Hansberry and Suzan-Lori Parks explore the terrains that depict black women's quest for identity and find it necessary to change the images and identities of black women created by the Whites and men. Empowering black women to define themselves on their own terms by negating the myths about them, Hansberry and Parks attempt to replace the image of black women from being victim of oppression to the ones who resist the subordination. They challenge the patriarchal and hierarchal system where Whites and men enjoy the privileges of high rank placing women and Blacks, especially black women in the lowest rung of the ladder of hierarchy.

The theme of quest for identity in black women is effectively employed by Lorraine Hansberry. Her women characters try to speak out against oppression to create a sense of individual identity in the face of silence, invisibility and absence from the mainstream discourses. Hansberry challenges patriarchal beliefs in *A Raisin in the Sun* where black women's free thinking is questioned and seen as a threat to the hegemonic order. What Maya Angelou says about women of all colours and in particular, for the ignored black women who need a voice reflects Hansberry's concerns: "So many young Black women are not spoken to by white women. Are not spoken to by Black men. Are not spoken to by white men. And if we don't speak there will be no voice reaching their ears or their hearts" (qtd. in Wisker 49).

Ruth, mother of Travis considers her power and control over her son, integral to her role as his mother, her only identity according to her. But when Travis doesn't obey her and is supported by his father Walter for doing so, Ruth senses a threat to her identity. Although she believes that being a woman and a mother, she should serve her family selflessly.

Beneatha is the one of those strong characters through whom Hansberry puts forth her feminist ideals. She is young and attractive college student who has an independent perspective of her own about things. Her aim to pursue her education and become a doctor reflects her urge to have an identity of her own. In 1950s, black female doctors could rarely be there and black women could not even think about such a prospect. But Beneatha does not let herself be pushed into accommodating to what was considered the norm. She leaves no stone unturned to continue her studies making it very clear to her brother and her suitors that it is not marriage that is her priority, but a successful career. She refuses to accept the subservient roles which are attributed to women and firmly asserts for her rights. She bluntly puts forth her view point to Asagai:

> BENEATHA: You never understood that there is more than one kind of feeling which can exist between a man and a woman— or, at least, there should be.
>
> ASAGAI: Ho. Between a man and a woman there need be only one kind of feeling. I have that for you...
>
> BENEATHA: I know—and by itself—it won't do. I can find that anywhere.
>
> ASAGAI: For a woman it should be enough.
>
> BENEATHA: I know— because that's what it says in all the novels that men write. But it isn't . . . I'm not interested in being someone's little episode in America. (64)

Cheney rightly offers an interpretation of her name: "Beneatha is an obvious pun, suggesting her contempt for many traditional ties" (qtd. in Gold 6). This bears out uncompromising attitude of Hansberry's heroine vis-à-vis her quest for identity as a black woman professional. She brushes aside all suggestions that conventionally limit women to perform roles of a mother, wife or sister. Through Beneatha, Hansberry attributes a sense of optimism and hopefulness in her women characters and thus, challenges the mundane portrayal of conservative views on womanhood by proving that women are equally good and strong as men are. Beneatha can be compared to Alice Walker who was also of the same opinion:

> Unlike many women who were told throughout their adolescence they must marry, I was never told by my mother or any one of her sisters it was something I need even think about. It is because of them that I know women can do anything, and that one's sexuality is not affected by one's work. (185)

The play also demolishes the myths of beauty perpetuated in the white world—particularly skin colour, facial features, and hair texture. Also children's rhyme often sung in black communities proclaims, "Now, if you're white you're all right, If you're brown, stick around, But if you're black, Git back! Git back! Git back!" (Collins 89). Hansberry depicts in the play the parameters of beauty as created by the white society and delves deep into the psyche of black women who are deeply affected by it but have learnt to interrogate such ideals. Beneatha believes that the texture of her hair is a defining feature of her identity. Hence, she prefers a look that represents her racial and cultural identity as a black woman. In the beginning of the play her hair is straight like white women's hair, but gradually she develops interest in her culture and decides to come closer to her culture by cutting her hair and wearing the look of traditional African American woman. She strongly believes natural is truly beautiful and black is beautiful too. This assertive step taken by Beneatha depicts her strong feminist perspective as a black woman. She stands by what she believes in, caring little what society thinks. She is happy to have her own identity— to be an African American following the traditional dressing style of her ancestors. Returning to her roots gives her a strong sense of her identity.

In *Venus,* the detailed physical description of the so-called Venus Hottentot depicts how black women are presented:

> Her hair was black and wooly, much like that of the common Negro, the slits of the eyes horizontal as in Mongols, not oblique . . . her lips blackish, terribly thick; her complexion very dark. Her ears were much like those found in monkeys . . . . Above all she had a way of pushing out her lips just like the monkeys do. (113)

Suzan-Lori Parks investigates specific questions of black women's experience and highlights the fact that black women are not only denigrated but also denied access to their rights and privileges which are provided to others. Parks underlines the notion of self-negation of a black woman. In her plays like *Venus, Pickling, Betting on the Dust Commander, Fucking A* and *In the Blood*, the playwright interrogates the African American selfhood in relation to men and white society. Specifically in her plays *In the Blood* and *Venus*, Parks recounts the black women's history by revealing the hidden evils of a racist and a patriarchal society. The plays highlight the roles society assigned to black women in love relationships and marriage. Her women characters attempt as well as succeed in obliterating the distorted and false images of black women formed by the Whites.

Imperceptible Mutabilities in the Third Kingdom, unfolds the saga of the long and arduous struggle of black people to reclaim their identity. The play consists of four parts with different titles and storyline but all of them show an unmistakable connection with the turbulent history of black people. Parks harks back to the past and tries to connect it with the present. Slavery had a devastating effect on a black woman's body as well as her mind. It deconstructed black women's self-identity by objectifying them or treating them as objects. Hence, they were dubbed as inferior to all. In part 1, "Snails," three women struggle to confirm their identity and humanity in the white world where they get animal like treatment. "The title ironically reinforces the characters' ineluctable, specimen-like relationship to their shelter" (Garret 13). Their original names are Molly, Charlene and Veronica. Their identities are trivialized by giving them homogeneous names— Mona, Chona and Verona. They face the loss of self. They repeatedly objectify themselves. Mona / Molly says, "Once there was uh me named Mona who wondered what she'd be like if no one was watching" (27). Maya Angelou once said:

> Every person I know had a hellish horror of being 'called out of his name.' It was a dangerous practice to call a Negro anything that could be loosely constructed as insulting because of the centuries of their having been called Niggers, Jigs, dinges, blackbirds, crows, boots and spooks. (qtd. in Wisker 50)

Suzan-Lori Parks deplores the mutability of black bodies by the white world. Molly uses the term 'mines' which points towards her identity, self and also her vulnerability. She even hesitates to claim her name. Faces 'otherness' without any identity of her own, victimhood dogs her. She is kicked out of her school just because of her inability to recite requisite lines from a version of "Mary Had a Little Lamb." She desperately wants to qualify the English test to remain in job but she is not able to make it. She is punished for not accepting and valorizing white codes and symbols. While opposing the manner in which her boss tries to impose on her the purposeless basic skills, she says, "Couldnt see thuh sense uh words workin like he said couldnt see the sense of workin . . . they tell me get Basic Skills call me breaking protocol . . . Think I'll splat?" (26). She is forced by her white teacher to unlearn her black heritage to erase her black identity. White society deconstructs the identity of girls as black women. Thus, black identity exists only in relation to white existence and self. Also, they are denied the right to put forth their viewpoint. Hence, their learning remains restricted. Molly is expelled by her white teacher for not remembering the correct way to pronounce words. Lutzsky, representative of white society erodes three black women's identity and dignity by being too intrusive. In other words, the white world dehumanizes these three black women and treats them as insects. Lutzsky bugs the apartment where Mona and Chona live. He places a tiny camera inside the roach and attempts to examine them as objects.

Likewise in another part of the play *Imperceptible Mutabilities in the Third Kingdom*, "Open House," Parks presents a black female servant, Aretha Saxon who faces the issue of being uprooted from her true self. She takes care of her master's children, Anglor and Blanca Saxon. She is an enslaved women who contemplates leaving her job as a caretaker owing to a highly restrictive environment. Arthea's identity, like Mona's and Chona's identities, completely rests in white people's hands. Miss Faith tells Arthea about her soon to be expired contract after which was as per the Emancipation Proclamation, she is supposed to be free. Arthea is asked to remove her teeth but when she resists, Miss Faith retorts that the teeth must be removed and photographed in order to be chronicled in the book of history. This illustrates that Whites had the power to extract the body parts of her (teeth) and disembody her without her consent. Thus, a black women's identity is defined in respect of her relationship with others or the creators of her identity. Also, in *In the Blood,* Hester feels the loss of her individual identity as her physical and emotional self is not acknowledged by the other character who exploits her sexually. She becomes just a source through which Doctor and Welfare official gratify their own sexual desires much against her will.

Womanist Bonding as Mothers and Sisters

While sharing their distinctive personal experiences, black feminists endeavour to transform and empower black women. Black feminists have attempted to repel the negative images of black women moving towards self-valuation and self-love. Black womanhood represents self-definition and self-worth of black women. Black Women writers have given a central place to black women's relationships with one another. Lorraine Hansberry and Suzan-Lori Parks give voice to their characters who have the ability to communicate powerfully— are insightful, supportive of sisterhood and women's creative potential which enables them to resist racism and sexism. The idea of sisterhood often refers to women's bonding, their participation in creative activities such as storytelling, quilting, singing together, etcetera. It implies that women relate to one another in ways that are totally different from how they relate to men. In her play, *A Raisin in the Sun*, she explores this theme in depth. She presents the love, care and affection that women share. The play depicts the great bonding between a mother-in-law and a daughter-in-law through the characters of Lena Younger and Ruth respectively. They deeply support and care for each other, which is evident in small things. Lena says to Ruth, "What's the matter with you this morning, Ruth? You looks right peaked. You aiming to iron all them things? Leave some for me. I'll get to 'em this afternoon" (40). Mama also speaks tenderly to Ruth:

> MAMA: Ruth Younger, what's the matter with you today? You look like you could fall over
>
> RUTH: I'm tired.
>
> MAMA: Then you better stay home from work today. (42)

When Ruth tells Lena that she will not let her baby come in this cruel world and will abort her, Lena is the only one who actually feels Ruth's pain as she herself had lost her baby once. She understands how painful it is for a mother to, in a way, kill her baby.

And when Mama is about to get the insurance money, everybody acts selfishly, nobody thinks about Mama except Ruth. She advises her to spend it on herself not on them and makes her realize that it is her money:

> RUTH: Now that's your money. It ain't got nothing to do with me. We all feel like that . . .
>
> RUTH: You know what you should do, Miss Lena? You should take yourself a trip somewhere. To Europe or South America or someplace. (43)

And when finally, Mama takes the decision to buy a house in an all-white neighbourhood, Ruth appreciates her step and supports her fully. She sides with Mama, although her husband, Walter wants to utilize this money for opening a liquor store. Ruth cherishes the dream of owning a nice house. Hansberry depicts through this play that only a woman can understand other woman's happiness and feelings. This idea is also further driven home through the portrayal of the relationship of Lena and her daughter, Beneatha:

> MAMA: . . . What's the matter?
>
> BENEATHA: Mama, George is a fool—honest
>
> . . . .
>
> MAMA: . . . you better not waste your time with no fools
>
> . . . .
>
> BENEATHA: Thank you.
>
> MAMA: For what?
>
> BENEATHA: For understanding me this time. (98)

It shows a mother's concern, care and love for her daughter. Black women always have a strong bonding in a community that becomes a source of their survival and emotional support. As Alice Walker has rightly said, "It is the black woman's words that have the most meaning for us, her daughters, because she, like us, has experienced life not only as a black person, but as a woman" (275).

While acknowledging her mother's heritage, Walker depicts how the legacy of her mother has helped her in understanding herself. She says, "Her face, as she prepares the art that is her gift, is a legacy of respect she leaves to me, for all that illuminates and cherishes life. She has handed down respect for the possibilities . . ." (242).

Alice Walker showcases her mother's generation of women, who were not allowed to express themselves, were in actuality the models of creativity for their future generations who have the opportunity to express their art. She gives due credit to the generations of black grandmothers and mothers who had burdened themselves to bring light in their children's lives.

Suzan-Lori Parks also incorporates the idea of sisterhood in her plays. In *Imperceptible Mutabilities in the Third Kingdom*, in part 1, subtitled "Snails", Molly/ Mona was in distress as she has failed in English test of basic skills and lost her job. Chona offers sympathy to Mona and tries to encourage her by telling her about a robber without speech, who made an attempt to steal Naturalist's giant spy-roach.

In *Fucking A*, Parks creates and invents a language, 'TALK' which is understood only by women in the play. It depicts a connection and solidarity between women irrespective of race and class. Women are empowered through a woman-specific language that enables them to voice their silence. It is also a language through which a woman understands women's issues and concerns:

> Weh noonk . . . rum— I missed my period. I stuck
>
> something up there, but—
>
> Weh nim . . . rum— I took one of them tests. Its
>
> said "not pregnant," but—
>
> Tah humble Yr showing
>
> Tah humble si Yr showing too. (224)

Black women's writings replace the historically constructed negative image of a mother as "mammy" figure with the real image of a strong motherhood. Motherhood is a shared responsibility involving caring, nurturing and strengthening. Motherhood signifies power rather than vulnerability of black women. Black women intellectuals portray African American mothers as courageous women with tremendous strength to deal with every situation and do everything for their families. It remains as an enduring theme in black women writing:

> The historical construction of the Black woman as the "great mother", negatively embedded in the "mammy" figure of Euro- American imagination, is confronted with the practical realities of mothering in recent Black women's writing. (Davies 99)

Concepts of matriarch, motherhood and womanhood have helped in changing the negative images of black women postured by the white media. Lorraine Hansberry's and Suzan-Lori Parks' plays are dominated by women. Mothers in their plays are dealt with great dignity and are so powerfully drawn that they captivate the audiences and readers. Hansberry in her plays, *A Raisin in the Sun* and *The Drinking Gourd* has epitomized motherhood through the relationship between mothers and children. She presents rebellious matriarchs namely Lena Younger and Rissa who symbolize the image of Mother Africa dismantling the negative image of an African mother perpetuated by dominating structures. Sharon Friedman observes:

> In periods when women's equality has been a powerful social issue, feminist concerns are central to plays by women. . . . Lena in *A Raisin in the Sun* and Rissa in *The Drinking Gourd* are not dramatizations of black women who emasculate black men. Rather, they are the ones who repudiate the negative images of black women as passive or destructive. . . . They are women "who contribute not only

> to the survival of their families and communities, but also to the active resistance often necessary to that survival. (qtd. in Leeson 147)

Rissa and Lena represent motherhood that is nurturing and enabling. Alice Walker, in *In Search of Our Mothers' Gardens*, refers to the creativity and power of black women that lay buried under the yoke of centuries of oppression:

> Yet so many of the stories that I write, that we all write, are my mother's stories . . . through years of listening to my mother's stories of her life, I have absorbed not only the stories themselves, but something of . . . the urgency that involves the knowledge that her stories like her life— must be recorded. (qtd. in Murphy157)

Parks' plays present the black female body, as caricatured and stereotyped which resembles historically racist images of the black female as Mammy, Jezebel and Breeder Woman. But at the same time, she also positions this body as the protagonist of each play and, in doing so, she raises a question about the validity of these stereotypes. Lorraine Hansberry also repudiates the prototypical black mammy image. They are courageous and rebellious but at the same time they are full of love and care. Both the plays show concerns of black women for the continuity of the peace and survival of the self and the family:

> Hansberry dedicated her best known play, *A Raisin in the Sun*, "to Mama: in gratitude for the dream." The heroic potential of motherhood finds its way into her plays through the strong presence of characters like Lena and Ruth Younger in *A Raisin in the Sun* and the slave mother Rissa in *The Drinking Gourd*. Hansberry's art shows a deep

> sensibility to the intricacies of women's lives under challenging, possibly devastating, social conditions. (Beaulieu 389)

A *Raisin in the Sun* is a milestone in Black Women's Drama. The play is powerfully sustained by the theme of motherhood. Motherhood in this play is represented through the character of Lena Younger. By virtue of her size and her title of "Mama Lena," Lena Younger is an imposing figure in the household. She controls her family in a manner that combines emotional and physical intimidation. Harris asserts, "Viewing her brand of domestic violence as acceptable in a culture that was well acclimated to the concept of the domineering black matriarch" (114). Lena does not want to control her children and grandson for the sake of maintaining power but she just wants to provide them growth and good opportunity. She always encourages her children to do something good and achieve something in their lives. She encourages her daughter, Beneatha to go to medical school and to realize her ambition of becoming a doctor. She fully supports her because she knows that this is the only way that her daughter can have a better future. She wishes a better life for Ruth, Walter and Travis as well. She buys the house so that her family has all the comforts. Her concern for little things is visible throughout the play. The following conversation bears it out:

> MAMA: I noticed all last week he had cold cereal, and when it starts getting this chilly in the fall a child ought to have some hot grits or something when he goes out in the cold—
>
> RUTH: I gave him oats—is that all right!

> MAMA:. . . . Put a lot of nice butter on it? He likes lots of butter. (41)

This shows that Lena takes care of small little things to ensure happiness of her children. When Ruth reaches home from hospital, Mama asks her whether everything is fine. She knows that women get depressed sometimes when they cannot have their way. She asks Ruth to relax and not to worry about anything. She tells her, "Come on now honey. You need to lie down and rest a while . . . then have some nice hot food" (60). Her behaviour towards Ruth depicts her motherly care and affection. The house with a backyard purchased out of insurance money is to fulfil her family's dream and a bid to retrieve the lost happiness of Younger family. The big yard would be a place where her grandson can play. Speaking to her son Walter, she says:

> Son. . . . I just seen my family falling apart today . . . just falling to pieces in front of my eyes. . . . We was going backwards' stead of forwards—talking 'bout killing babies and wishing each other was dead . . . When it gets like that in life—you just got to do something bigger. . . . I wish you'd say how deep inside you think I done the right thing. (94)

She feels that possibly her son had different dreams. However, her large-heartedness and sensitivity in dealing with things show her wisdom and selflessness both:

> MAMA: Listen to me . . . I say I been wrong, son. That I been doing to you what the rest of the world been doing to you. . . . There ain't nothing worth holding on to, money, dreams, nothing else—if it means—if it means it's going to destroy my boy. . . . I paid the man thirty five hundred

dollars down on house. That leaves sixty five hundred dollars. Monday morning I want you to take this money and take three thousand for Beneatha's medical schooling. The rest you put in a checking account—with your name on it.

> WALTER: *(Stares at the money)* You trust me like that, Mama?

> MAMA: I ain't never stop trusting you. Like I ain't never stop loving you. (107)

Hansberry invests Mama's character with an inherent dignity and compassion. She gives Walter the remainder of the insurance money so as to help Walter out of his desolation. Although all the money belongs to Mama, being the insurance money, she got after her husband's death, she does not use it to fulfil her personal needs but she spends the whole amount on her children. She comes across as a mother who is self-sacrificing. Her influence on Ruth is profound. Ruth wants to give the best life to her son, Travis. She works as a domestic in white people's houses, even when she is sick, just to earn more money and secure a better life for her son. When Mama buys the house, Ruth expresses her immense happiness as the family would finally own a house. When Walter tells her that he has lost all the money by giving it to Willy, Mama's hopes are crushed and she tells Ruth that they will not be moving now. At this Ruth pleads before her to make the move because she does not want to miss the only opportunity to provide a good atmosphere and a proper house to her child. She says, "Lena—I'll work. . . . I'll strap my baby on my back if I have to scrub all the floors in America and wash all the sheets . . . but we got to MOVE! We got to get OUT OF HERE" (140). A mother's resolve to do anything for the happiness and good future of her child is evident in not only Mama's efforts but also Ruth's strong will in the face of utter poverty and deprivation. One encounters images of strong women who refuse to become victims of circumstances. On the contrary, they take decisions that empower them and their families.

Lena is a religious woman and her religion is a source of power to deal with the problems in her life. As it is her responsibility as a mother to inculcate moral values in her children, she never misses a chance to incorporate her religious ideals into their lives. And violation of moral values is not tolerated by her. This is evident when Beneatha is slapped by her for saying that there is no God and she does not believe in God. At this Mama asks her to repeat after her what she says:

> MAMA: Now–you say after me, in my mother's house there is still God In my mother's house there is still God.
>
> BENEATHA: In my mother's house there is still God. (51)

She feels that no child borne of her body could have strayed so far from the moral values of their mother. Similar is her reaction towards Walter, when she comes to know that he wants to invest the insurance money in the liquor store. She feels it is morally wrong to make money by selling alcohol to their already oppressed community. In the last act, when Walter refuses Lindner to accept his offer, Lena feels great that her values still reside somewhere inside her children. Walter proves that for him nothing is more important than his family's peace and welfare. He prefers love above any personal material gains. This reflects that Mama's values are deeply embedded in her children's lives.

Since Lena has always inculcated among her children values of love, affection and respect for others; hence, any departure from good behaviour and kindness enrages her. When she finds her children fighting, she loses her temper:

> MAMA: Yes— death done come in this here house. . . . walking in my house on the lips of my children. You–what supposed to be my beginning again. You—what supposed to be my harvest . . . you mourning your brother? (144)
>
> She adds:
>
> What you tell him a minute ago? That he wasn't a man?. . . . You done wrote his epitaph too— like the rest of the world? Well, who give you the privilege?
>
> BENEATHA: Be on my side for once! You saw what he just did, Mama! You saw him— down his knees. Wasn't it you who taught me to despise any man who would do that.
>
> MAMA: Yes— I taught you that. . . . But I thought I taught you something else too . . . I thought I taught you to love him.
>
> BENEATHA: Love him? There is nothing left to love.
>
> MAMA: There is always something left for love. And if you ain't learned that, you ain't learned nothing. (145)

Mama's motherly feelings are also reflected in her concern for Beneatha's friend Asagai. She treats him like her own son Walter. She assumes that he needs a nurturing mother's love. Hence, she asks him to come to their place anytime without any hesitation to enjoy the taste of decent home cooked meals:

MAMA: How many miles is it from here to where you come from?

ASAGAI: Many thousands.

MAMA: I bet you don't half look after yourself, being away from your mama. . . . you better come round here from time to time to get yourself some decent home-cooked meals . . .

ASAGAI: (*Moved*) Thank you. Thank you very much. (65)

Mama is a supportive and nurturing mother, characteristics that are usually associated with African American mothers.

In *The Drinking Gourd*, Hansberry shows what it means to love as a mother and be a black American mother. Rissa is also an equally powerful woman, who has instilled the right values in her children. In the beginning we see Rissa convincing Hannibal to work at Hiram's house so that he will not have to work in the fields. A mother always wants the best things in the world for her children but Rissa is a poor mother; still she tries her level best to give her children a comfortable life. She says pleadingly to Hannibal that one thing she had planned was that you and Isaiah would work in the Big House where they can get decent food and nice things to wear and learn nice manners like real gentlemen. As a mother's concern she has already secured him a position in the main house:

RISSA: Speakin' of boys, Marster Sweet, ain't you forgot about a certain promise in the last couple of months?

HIRAM: Oh, Rissa, Maria says she won't have it.

RISSA: Marster, a promise is a promise! And you promise me born he wasn't never gona have to be no field hand . . .

HIRAM: But we need all the hands in the fields we've got and Maria says there is absolutely nothing for another house servant to do around here.

RISSA: He kin do a little bit of everything. He kin help me in kitchen and Harry some in the house. He's gettin' so unruly, Marster Hiram. And you promised me—

HIRAM: All right, for God's sake! Anything for peace in this house! . . . Hannibal is a house servant. (187-88)

Hansberry crafts the slave master relationship of Rissa and Hiram as one of interdependence over the years on the plantation. But Rissa does not lose time to end this relationship, when she comes to know that Hiram's son Everet has punished her son so harshly for a petty cause and Hiram could not do anything in stopping his son from doing that.

In act 3, Rissa's simple, human, motherly act of vengeance for a son wronged depicts to what extent a woman can go when it comes to helping her child. Rissa turns her back on the dying master, Hiram Sweet, who had always given her a privileged position among the slaves, when she comes to know that he is the one responsible for blinding his son, even though indirectly. Hannibal's only crime was that he wanted and learnt to read and write, and is blinded for that. When Hiram enters Rissa's place to see her and her son and says that he will send for Dr. Bullett to tend to Hannibal, Rissa refuses and says that she herself can take care of her son. But when Hiram keeps on insisting, Rissa asks him whether a doctor can put his eyes back? Hiram judges her anger and says:

> HIRAM: I—I wanted to tell you, Rissa—I wanted to tell you and ask you to believe me that I had nothing to do with this. I—somethings do seem to be out of the power of my hands after all . . .
>
> RISSA: Why? Ain't you Marster? How can a man be marster of some men and not at all of others—
>
> HIRAM: You go too far—
>
> RISSA: Oh—? What will you have done to me? Will your overseer gouge out my eyes too? . . . . I done seen all there was worth seein' in this world—and it didn't mount to much. I think this talkin' disturb my boy. (215)

Hiram leaves a dejected and a defeated figure and suddenly collapses outside the cabin. He cries for help, tries to get back to Rissa's cabin but Rissa ignores him and looks out of the window to have a glimpse of a man whose cries for help she can distinctly hear. But she does not help Hiram and returns to Hannibal's bedside to take care of him. In effect, she murders him—and not only that, she steals his guns and hands these over to her children. This shows that an always forgiving mother will never forgive a person who destroys her child. Jeanne-Marie A. Miller discusses Hansberry's play and says:

> While Rissa has some of the characteristics of the "unrealistic mammy." She is also concerned about her own family. In various actions, Hansberry's slave mother "reverses the myth of the faithful, contented slave," who is happy in her servitude. Ultimately riveting her attention on

> her son, Rissa lets her master die outside her cabin. (499-500)

According to Friedman:

> Hansberry shatters the image of the black mammy. The play's matriarch, Rissa plays an active role in raising determined, rebellious sons. In author's view, the actions of Hansberry's mother refute the stereotypes that label black women as either passive or emasculating. (76)

Rissa leads to the completion of the journey that Lena had started on— and thereby literally reverses the stereotypical sacred image of the Black Mammy who is patient, long-suffering, devoted and indomitable, and above all loving and forgiving.

The theme of motherhood is a prominent theme in Suzan-Lori Parks' *Fucking A* and *In the Blood.* The central idea of the play, *Fucking A* is a mother's unwavering love for her child. In the play, women are seen aborting their babies which points to the historical fact that during slavery black women preferred to terminate their babies instead of giving them a life of servitude. Hester, an abortionist is depicted as the one living in the era of racism who looks upon motherhood as her only strength. She is living, earning and working just for the sake of her son who is prisoned falsely by a rich woman. She scraps and saves everything so that she can just have a picnic with her son. She works hard to free him. When the collection agency asks Hester to pay double the amount to see her son, she does not give up and instead continues to work harder towards her solitary goal. Parks portrays Hester as both a formidable and an extremely miserable figure who feels ashamed of her profession but reassures that it is the only way to free her son from prison. The irony is that society has created such a situation, where a mother has to strive to buy her child's freedom. The play, thereupon depicts that due to poverty and illiteracy of black women, the ones in power control them socially, economically and physically.

Similarly, in *In the Blood*, Parks brings to the forefront the theme of motherhood. Hester's deep love for her children recalls the Black mother figure, always seen as loving, caring, protecting, nurturing and self-sacrificing. Although the chorus calls Hester's five fatherless children as 'BASTARDS', but Hester calls them her five 'TREASURES' who have given meaning to her life:

> Jabber: You aint hungry?
>
> Hester: I'll eat later.
>
> Jabber: You always eating later. . . .
>
> Jabber/Bully/Trouble/Beauty/Baby
>
> Hester: Bedtime.
>
> Bully: Can we have a story?
>
> Hester: All right. (18-19)

After feeding her children, she tells them tales so as to make them sleep. Amiga mocks her for being a self-sacrificing mother who is always committed to her kids and neglects herself. Amiga, who herself makes money by selling her babies without feeling guilty, tries to drag Hester into the same by convincing her to follow her way—to use her body to get money. But Hester prefers her treasures over money. Parks explodes the myth of long suffering matriarch, when she depicts in her *Red Letter Plays* (*In the Blood* and *Fucking A*) that both the mothers in the plays kill their own sons to prevent them from facing more tragic ending.

Parks parts away a bit from the idealized icons of motherhood which is a cultural construct of femininity. Parks places the mothers on the margin of human experience where they become both victims and killers as a result of societal and cultural pressure where both of them failed to survive. Counterstatement of their characters is reflected through the two sides of their person, nurturing and caring mothers on one hand and murderers putting their children to death. Successive abuses and atrocities lead both the mothers to kill their own children, though their motives are different. Jon Dietrick sums up their predicament:

> Both plays end with the protagonist killing her own son, and while there are important contextual differences between the two killings, in each case this final act ironically underscores a tragic lack of agency on the part of the heroine. And in the end of both plays, neither the heroine's own situation nor social structures with which she clashes has changed significantly. (88-89)

Hester in *In the Blood* kills her son Jabber as he repeats the word 'slut' which he has always refused to do so in order to protect his mother's sentiments. This act of Jabber depicts that he no longer cares for her like all others in her life.

Likewise, Hester in *Fucking A* slits the throat of her son Monster but only after his request. Monster was about to be caught and tortured to death by hunters. She saved her son from a worse situation. Hunters' attitude is so merciless that Monster prefers to die rather than be hunted by them. As Monster says to his mother, "When they catch me theyll hurt me. Run me through and plant me in yr front yard so you can hear me scream . . . Us killing me is better than them killing me. . . . " (218–19). Hester is hesitant to kill her son, while Monster is waiting for his mother to act but finally, she makes up her mind to slit the throat of her own child using a method Butcher taught her, which is least painful. She says, "I have a way to do it that wont hurt. Give me yr knife. Sit in my lap" (219). In effect the mothers in both the plays do not kill their sons but they endeavour to kill an ideology constructed by the society. Jabber and Monster become what society makes them.

In this manner, *The Red Letter plays* suggest a pessimistic view of helplessness and inability of human beings to control their own lives. It would not be wrong to say that both the Hesters are created and later destroyed by their own world and society.

Alice Walker's idea of 'Womanism' refers to solidarity between black men and women as they strive for survival. It justifies the role and equal participation of a black man/woman in the struggle for obtaining equality and betterment of their future. Hansberry and Parks emphasize that men and women must fight the battle against racial, gender and class disparities together as their struggle is same. By portraying black women's movement from subjugation to resistance and assertion, they have rearticulated the idea of womanhood. Women always remain central to the plays of both the playwrights. Hansberry expresses through her plays, a deep sensitivity to the complexities of women's lives under challenging and difficult situations, representing them in a very dignified manner. Her women characters are revolutionary and courageous. Suzan Lori Parks too in her *Red Letter Plays* portrays the struggle of strong black women who speak out against their suffering and economic problems. Her plays showcase, like Lorraine Hansberry's drama, the experiences and concerns of the black women that originate from the intersectionality of race, gender and class and the man-woman relationship. She focuses on how black men and black women unite together to fight for their rights and this unity is one of the significant themes in her plays. Womanism encompasses issues that are important to African American women beyond those that concern white feminism. Black women focus is black women's culture, the family and combating racism together with men.

Suzan-Lori Parks understates the male/female dichotomy by showcasing the unity in black man and black woman through her play *The Death of the last man in the Whole Entire World* in which Black Woman with Fried Drumstick always stands by her husband. Even in his absence, she retaliates against the unjust execution of her husband and resists the orders she receives from white oppressors. As she says in panel I, "Comin for tuh take you. Told me tuh pack up your clothes. Told me tuh cut my bed in 2 from double tuh single. . . . I didnt do squat. . . . You comed back" (105). Black Man tells his histories/stories of oppression and retaliation to his wife as he thinks of his wife as a trustworthy companion and firmly believes that his survival is dependent on her. Black Woman takes up the responsibility to uphold the history and memory of their race about which Black Man with Watermelon is concerned. Nicole Hodges Persley says:

> She becomes representative of the strong black woman archetype … Parks positions Black Woman with Fried Drumstick as the narrator of story, a wife who is charged with supporting her husband and with being a leader in the community that surrounds her. (69)

Parks creates cohesion between African American men and women and exemplifies an active discursive role of African American women in racial uplift.

One of the important distinctions between white feminism and womanism is their attitude towards men. Womanists are more inclusive and consider men as partners in the battle against white racism and domination. This idea is driven home in the plays of Hansberry. In *A Raisin in the Sun*, at the end the whole family, both black men and women unite together to fight against the cruelty perpetrated on them by the Whites. They all decide to move to the white locality where they have bought a house, in spite of the threats. Although Walter needs money to fulfil his dreams, yet he prefers the dreams of his family including those of his mother, wife and sister. Similar bonding is visible in the other play, *The Drinking Gourd*. In this play the mother Rissa unites with her son Hannibal to combat the white discrimination. She takes her revenge by not attending to her white master, Hiram and by letting him die. In the last scene, Rissa is seen giving Hiram's gun to the blind Hannibal whom she helps to escape. Thus, she ultimately unites with his son to escape from the tyranny of the Whites.

According to hooks:

> [T]he necessary healing process is in the wake of damaging psychological assaults by whites will involve black self-love. This self- love or ethic of care gives primacy to the relationship between black females and males. . . . Resistance can be achieved when the toxic presence of white racism is eclipsed by an "ontological" blackness that black males and females can produce in their solidarity. (qtd. in West 162)

In *Les Blancs* by Lorraine Hansberry, though there is no such black female character in the play, the playwright does not marginalize the black woman's presence as well as her participation in the struggle for freedom. The black woman warrior, who symbolizes Africa, acts as a catalyst in anti-colonial revolution. She doesn't speak but her gestures have an equal significance if not more than words. She mimes the years of slavery and slaughter while representing Africa's uproar to be protected from atrocities like rape and exploitation at the hands of colonizers. Hansberry refigures a divergent rendition of womanhood through the black woman warrior/dancer by emphasizing on her strong presence even in her absence. She ignites Tshembe's call to revolutionary consciousness. In act 1, scene 3, she insistently and rigidly summons him: "she sweeps up the spear and halts, holding it vertical before her. . . . She holds it rigid for an instant, then tosses it, still vertical, to him, and he catches it instinctively" (81). Thus, her self-assertion propels Tshembe to the decision to join the growing revolution.

Reasserting themselves and Breaking the Silence

Audre Lorde says in the poem quoted by Gloria Hull at the opening of Conditions Five:

> Whether we speak or not,
>
> The machine will crush us to bits—
>
> And we will also be afraid
>
> Your silence
>
> will not protect you. (qtd. in Walker 283)

Twentieth century black feminist voices finally began to make themselves heard. The silenced and marginalized women began to celebrate women's community, paying heed to societal concerns and issues that arise from black women's real-life experiences. Having been categorized inferior, their identity and existence eroded under the influence of triple burden of race, caste and gender oppression. Black women were viewed as incapable of holding any responsibility and were excluded from public matters and therefore castigated, disempowered and silenced. Anna Cooper comments on the status of black women: "The white woman could at least plead for her own emancipation; the black woman doubly enslaved could but suffer and struggle and be silent" (qtd. in hooks 15-16). The best known African American women writers such as Toni Morrison, Alice Walker, Maya Angelou and many more asserted to bring to the forefront the hidden and silenced voices from the realm of history. They walked towards awareness and recognition and broke the silence of black women in order to explore their potential and to empower them.

Black women writers pay heed to the urge of the revolutionary transformation which is only possible if black women deliberately break their silence and invisibility by resisting the varied existing oppressions like whiteness, maleness and cultural codes. The oppressors deny the black women right to selfhood and speech to articulate and express their feelings. Lorraine Hansberry and Suzan-Lori Parks dig out the silenced voices of black women which were suppressed by white hegemony. Their plays while underscoring oppression, also highlight how black women turn from being passive to being resistant subjects who assert their rights and affirm their position in their own community as well as in the American society. Most of the women characters in the plays of Hansberry and Parks break their silence and rearticulate their unheard voices in order to redefine themselves.

Parks challenges the traditional construction of femininity. Her female protagonists refuse to limit themselves to the traditionally prescribed subservient roles. They resist the idealized icon of femininity that was prominent in history. Representation of black body throughout African American literature depicts strength and assertion for power. Parks uses the concept of agency which is integral to postcolonialism. Venus utilizes her sexuality to gain some kind of agency. Venus finds herself economically insecure and tries to exploit her black body/ seduction for material gain. To get fame and economic stability, she chooses to become an exotic dancer as she believes that by staging her sexuality, she will be able to erase false perceptions of its abomination. "Agency is particularly important in post-colonial theory because it refers to the ability of post-colonial subjects to initiate action in engaging or resisting imperial power" (Ashcroft et al. 6).

Parks challenges the traditional narrative of representation of black women by questioning the intersection of multiple oppressions. She presents strong-minded and independent women in her plays who have the will power to retaliate against the wrong done to them.

Likewise, the recurrent note of assertion is manifest in Lorraine Hansberry's plays as well. Hansberry does not portray her women characters as an inarticulate and pitiable but the ones having a voice of their own. They embody traits that represent black womanhood such as audacity, wisdom and endurance.

In *Raisin in the Sun*, Beneatha is determined to attain her individuality and not to be defined by the man she marries. In the end, Beneatha's decision to marry Asagai symbolizes her self-assertion and independence. She chooses Asagai over Murchison as Asagai respects African culture and he is also willing to take Beneatha's career goals seriously. Brenda F. Berrian observes, "Focus on the theme of interracial marriage between Beneatha and Joseph Asagai in *A Raisin in the Sun* can be viewed as a testimony of self-assertion, new freedom and a positive step towards black identity" (qtd. in Leeson 151). Ruth's decision to abort her baby is taken solely by her, as she realizes that it is her body and she has full right to take the decision. In 1959, abortion was considered illegal; Hansberry makes a bold feminist statement through her character Ruth. Diana Adesola Mafe says, "Ruth maintains her ostensibly natural "right to choose" whether or not to have an abortion, an extreme "prerogative" reminiscent of the black woman's agency during slavery" (qtd. in Bloom 138).

Both the playwrights place women at the centre of the narrative by foregrounding their genuine experiences, their resistance and triumphs. As Audre Lorde puts it, "writing enables women to speak out, step out and value their lives" (qtd. in Wisker 38). Lorraine Hansberry's and Suzan-Lori Parks' drama is about African American ethos. Through their plays they bring to the fore the quintessential issues that highlight the exclusiveness of the black American community and actually articulate the suppressed voice of black women by "speaking" to them.

3
Born Black: Racism and Slavery

Post colonialism is far from being the term which means demise of colonialism, but it can be viewed as a protest against the colonial rule and domination. It deals with the history of anti-colonial resistance against dominant western culture. African Americans share a history of colonial exploitation as they were firstly marginalized and then isolated from their history, culture and native land. Post colonialism became a place where culture, identity and history are reassessed, re-created and re-defined universally. Since the colonial era, particularly in the United States, racism and ethnic discrimination have been major issues, the heavy burden of which has been borne by African Americans for a very long time.

Tracing the history of racial oppression, it becomes evident that racism was the driving force behind the transatlantic slave trade. Slavery and segregation are the most painful historical eras and are the major racially structured institutions. Perhaps the institution of slavery under which African Americans were enslaved and were ill-treated by an inhuman regime, is the most prominent form of American racism.

The transatlantic slave trade resulted in the most coercive migration of a large human population in history. During the period of 1700-1800, millions of Africans were transported to North and South America, the European nations, the Caribbean and many other nations. Africans' lives were changed drastically. They were forced to live as slaves for centuries in America and were treated like animals. Working from sunrise to sunset and that too without pay, they often became victims of violence of slave owners who would beat, starve and even whip them. In the early nineteenth century, Whites of all social classes had the legal right to work for pay but the majorities of Blacks were still enslaved and were deprived of any citizenship rights. Whites advocated the enslavement of Blacks in many ways as they believed that blackness of skin reflected evil and hence slave trade was justified. In fact Whites' own identity rested upon how they defined Blacks.

Slavery / Slave Narratives

Philip Schwarz says, "One origin of the word slave is the medieval Latin Sclavus, which not only means "slave" but also "slav." The Slavs were people of eastern Europe who were conquered in the 800s and often sold as slaves" (qtd. in Kachur 5). Slavery as an established institution has existed in human societies since 1776 when the nation came into being. In the United States the native Africans and African Americans were enslaved under the system of chattel enslavement, which was legalized. As per law, an enslaved person was treated as a commodity or property. This form of slavery lasted officially till 1865, with the Thirteenth Amendment of the constitution of America. Slavery, however, continued to exist as an institution associated with the race and colour of the skin of the people of African descent.

The slave narratives document the first-hand experiences of the slaves primarily in the American South. In the 1840s and 1850s, the people of colour began to record their struggles in the face of disparities between American ideal of so-called freedom and the sordid reality of racism. As the American Civil War came to an end, former slaves continued to narrate their agonizing experiences. They wrote to ensure that the newly-united nation does not forget as to what had threatened its existence, and also to remind readers of their contribution to social and economic progress.

Slave-narratives are significant precursors of the African American literary tradition and culture. Until the Depression of the 1930s and the years that followed, the number of slave narratives exceeded the number of novels written by African Americans. Among the classics of American literature, the influence of the slave narratives can be seen on many path-breaking nineteenth-century American novels including Harriet Beecher Stowe's *Uncle Tom's Cabin* (1852), Mark Twain's *Huckleberry Finn* (1884), William Styron's *The Confessions of Nat Turner* (1967) and Toni Morrison's *Beloved* (1987). Slave narratives played a major role in discourse on slavery and racism that shook the conscience of the United States.

At the same time the slave narratives also served to acquaint the white readers about the true nature of the institution of slavery. They also highlight the fact that slavery accorded a sub-human status to the black people and that they deserve full human rights as individuals. There have been attempts to dismiss the slave narratives as mere propaganda. However, their popularity the world over bears out their significance in society and literature. In fact, their power as documents that still continue to generate reflection and debate on questions of race, justice, inequities and freedom is unparalleled. It is true that the writers of slave narratives had faced many impediments when they advocated the abolition of slavery. In the nineteenth century many writers like Fredric Douglas, W.E.B. Du Bois and Marcus Garvey came up with texts to enhance black education and black development and endeavoured to place emphasis on the ideals of their ancestors.

Slave narratives shed light on the violence and atrocities perpetrated on the Blacks and serve as tools in the formation and exploration of the new African American identity. These tales narrate the brutal treatment of the Blacks at the hands of the Whites after they were sold and made to work far away from their families and coerced to lead undignified lives in poverty. While in captivity, they were also forced to imbibe the western culture. The native Africans were also instrumental in encouraging the slave trade. African abolitionist Ottabah Cugoano was also sold into slavery in the mid- 1700s. Acknowledging the role of the West Africans in slave trade, he once said, "I must own to the shame of my countrymen that I was first kidnapped and betrayed by [people of] my own complexion" (qtd. in Kachur 50). Another abolitionist Olaudah Equiano also known as Gustavus Vassa worked to end slavery. He was also enslaved at the age of 11. In 1789, he wrote his life story entitled, *The Interesting Narrative of the life of Olaudah Equiano* which reflects the slaves' perspective on how it feels to be enslaved. He also wrote about the barbarous and inhuman treatment of Blacks aboard the slave ship. Equiano's narrative was deeply engrained in the traditions contributing to antislavery writing. He describes his experiences about being kidnapped and sold to the slave traders. Describing the brutal scene aboard a slaver, he says "The white people looked and acted, as I thought, in so savage a manner; for I had never seen among any people such instances of brutal cruelty" (qtd. in Bruce Jr. 90). The slave narratives contributed to both the larger African American literary canon and the American literary canon. The slave narratives published in the 18th and 19th centuries helped the classes of power, those who were educated to initiate social change in regard to slavery.

Throughout history, white masters imposed legal ownership over Blacks who were bought and then kept in bondage. After New Jersey's act for the Gradual Abolition of Slavery, African Americans gradually began to show resistance towards oppression. Initiatives were taken towards developing African American churches and educational institutions with white leadership as well as by African Americans themselves. Such developments were taken as signs of progress and a hope for the ensuing generation of Blacks throughout the North of America. However, all these positive signs were absent in South:

> On the eve of the abolition of the slave trade, importation reached significant levels: the number of slaves imported in the decade before closure was virtually double that of the preceding decade. The domestic trade continued without abatement. (Bruce Jr. 93)

Southern states remained staunchly conservative regarding eradication of slavery. Blacks were denied access to public institutions. "The Southern states declared themselves as an independent country, the Confederate State of America… They wrote their own constitution which said that slavery was legal everywhere in their country" (Kachur 100). Thus, slavery was more deeply rooted in the Southern States than in the North of America.

Long before 1865 when the Civil War ended, Blacks were liberated but their freedom was not guaranteed and they continued to suffer from the tyranny of the Whites. Even in the North in many areas there was a severe curtailing of economic opportunities for the Blacks. Various institutional practices, cultural representations and rules perpetuated racial inequality in the society. Blacks officially got freedom but were categorized as inferior and were subjected to humiliations. Jim Crow laws were enacted during 1980s in response to the abolition of the slave system after Civil War. According to these laws segregation between Blacks and Whites was legalized. Consequently, it relegated the African Americans to the status of second class citizens thus resulting in minimizing any opportunities for them. Blacks got the worst schools, hospitals and other public institutions. Besides, the threat of losing their jobs and even lynching loomed large before them if they dared to protest. Jim Crow laws increased the discrimination against Blacks. African Americans were thus subjected to follow particular rules and regulations and were denied freedom.

Writing is invariably an expression of the deepest of the impulses of any section of humanity. African American writers endeavoured through their works to express black identity and liberty. They brought black experiences to the forefront as serious dramas and thus (re)defined the American theatre that had set up conventional ways and formed typical images of Blacks. Racial history holds a special place in Lorraine Hansberry's and Suzan-Lori Parks' plays as they portray the historical experience of Blacks through the construction of themes like slavery, poverty and violence. Their works foreground the values, beliefs, social ambience, political atmosphere and culture of African Americans exploring the faded history of black experiences and attempts to present it by recreating it through different perception.

Lorraine Hansberry's was a powerful voice. She stood and spoke for those who experienced pain and degradation due to racial discrimination. Her interest in the divisive class issues between Blacks and Pan-Africanism as a political and cultural movement was deep. In 1951, she joined the *Freedom* newspaper which gave her an opportunity to work with W.E.B. Du Bois. She began to focus on the lives, experiences and politics of black people throughout the world with a revolutionary spirit:

> It is safe to say that in Hansberry's intellectual and emotional involvement in the plight of oppressed black people, this bright independent woman in a man's world began to feel acutely and empathize with the oppression of others in various social circumstances which placed them "outside" the prevailing majority, often making them victims of sexism and bigotry. (Leeson 8)

From the very beginning of her career as a writer Hansberry had been quite courageous and revolutionary. Activism was a part of Hansberry family life. Her parents were intellectuals and activists. Her father was an active member of the Republican Party. Lorraine became not only an eminent and powerful writer who wrote for the rights of Blacks in her works but also as a social activist who had a revolutionary zeal to reform the society. She belonged to a privileged class but always felt deeply for the oppressed class. She struggled to break the barriers of racism in order to create the most essential social change even marrying interracially which was against the norm. She joined the organizations like Young Progressives of America and Labour Youth League that fought for racial equality. Hansberry's fame as a dramatist established her as a champion for the cause of civil rights. She became active in the Civil Rights Movements in the South and spoke at rallies as an activist artist on behalf of those who led oppressed lives. She had always rejected the limits imposed on her race and never supported the separation of classes among Blacks that would give importance to certain groups, while majority of them still lived in poverty and were subject to racial violence. Being the granddaughter of a freed slave, she continued to deeply devote herself to the black struggle for equality and human rights and in the process became a spokesperson for black Americans. Her concerns and views against racism and discrimination are strongly reflected in her literary works.

Hansberry's plays address at every point the structural edifice where slaves' pain and suffering are reflected. In *A Raisin in the Sun*, *Les Blancs* and *The Drinking Gourd*, she demonstrates the devastating effects of slavery. These works depict how the Blacks' dignity was often trampled by the Whites. Hansberry also highlights their economic oppression and cruelty they were subjected to. At the same time, she also showcases the dreams and the aspirations of Blacks and the consequent assertion by them. In *Les Blancs*, Hansberry presents one of the most powerful discourses on the meaning of race. Building on the dynamics of race relations and colonialism, the play depicts that the race is conditional and is socially constructed. Hansberry intends to explore the historical grounding of oppression and the revolt against it in Africa. The play deals with the political upheavals and unrest in Africa and urge for self-determined identity. The protagonist of the play, Tshembe Matoseh returns from abroad for his father's funeral who was the leader of a resistance movement against colonial rule. Tshembe used to live in Europe and is now pulled apart between his new life in Europe and his responsibility towards his people and place. He finally resolves the dilemma by deciding to live permanently in Africa to liberate his people by becoming an active participant of resistance movement. He has always been supported by his brother Eric, who was born of an interracial rape when his mother was assaulted by Major Rice, a white man. She had died while giving birth to Eric. "Eric was the living denial of everything he stood for: the testament to three centuries of rape and self-acquittal" (125). Eric has a revolutionary spirit and is highly determined to fight against colonialism.

A Raisin in the Sun deals with the suffering of an African American family. Slavery is one of the major issues in this play. Hansberry has depicted how five generations of an African American family had been serving the Whites without any counteraction. They had come to accept it as their malevolent destiny. As Lena, the mother tells her son Walter Lee, "So—I come from five generations of people who was slaves and sharecroppers" (143). Three members of Younger family are still leading the lives of slaves. Lena and Ruth are domestic servants who look after others' children and work in others' kitchens. Walter Lee, the male character is a chauffeur.

Lorraine Hansberry has also dealt with the turmoil of slavery in her other play, *The Drinking Gourd.* In this play, Lorraine brings out the essential view of "the realities of the time," that is the pain of being a slave. It unfolds the saga of oppression, deep agony and brutality faced by the Blacks. The play unveils the slaves' treatment by their white masters who treat Blacks not as human beings but consider them as their personal properties and deprive them of the basic human rights. The tyranny of Whites is revealed throughout the play. Blacks are exploited as there were no fixed working hours, no guaranteed minimum wages and no trade unions. The narrator describes how labour is so plentiful in the south that it might be cheaper to work a man to death and then buy another rather than to treat him less harshly so he will last.

The horrors of the slave trade that brought the slaves to America are very well described by the narrator. He points out that in the nineteenth century, child labour in the north was a norm, women were not considered equal citizens and the mentally ill were punished for their madness.

Giving expression to heart wrenching emotions of the black slaves, the slavery songs hold a vital position in Blacks' plays as they eternalize the oral tradition of black community by communicating the histories and stories of Blacks and their homeland. Slaves used to sing a song where they plead to their gods for help:

> Bornu-land was rich and good,
>
> Wells of water, fields of food,
>
> Bornu land me see no longer,
>
> Here we thirst and here we hunger
>
> Here the Moor man smiles in anger
>
> Where are we going Rubee?. . . .
>
> Hear us, save us, Rubee!. . . .
>
> Hear us! Tell us where are we going? (qtd. in Kachur 61)

Slavery songs reflect the emotional experience, joy and sorrows of slaves. They provide slaves a relief from mental tension. Lorraine Hansberry and Suzan-Lori Parks have extensively used slave songs in their works which throw light on the bitter realities of the slave system.

Lorraine Hansberry has made use of two songs: 'Follow the Drinking Gourd' and 'Steal away to Jesus' in her play, *The Drinking Gourd*. Both the songs suggest escape from slavery and are used to signalize secret messages to each other. The title of the play *The Drinking Gourd* has a deeper meaning and in itself unfolds the plight of slaves. It throws light on what drinking gourd meant to the slaves and how important it was for them to escape the harsh reality of life. The title itself has been taken from a spiritual song, "Follow the Drinking Gourd," a song of Underground Railroad which is derived from old slave metaphor for the Big Dipper which hints to North star, a symbol of freedom for many escaped slaves who want to make a way towards North. Hansberry has focused on the dream of freedom, along with the right to be accepted and treated as a human being. In the very beginning of act 1, the desire for freedom is very well portrayed through a song:

> Steal away, steal away,
>
> Steal away to Jesus.
>
> Steal away steal away home—
>
> I ain't got long to stay here.
>
> My Lord he calls me,
>
> He calls me by the thunder.
>
> The trumpet sounds
>
> within-a my soul—
>
> I ain't got long to stay here. (168)

Hannibal, the protagonist of the play expresses his dream to escape from this tyrannical world where Blacks are not treated as human beings but like machines subjected to work for long hours. Hannibal's brother Isaiah has escaped to North. After his wife is sold, he is left with no choice but to escape to North to secure his freedom and that of his wife's after earning money. Hannibal also plans and dreams to do the same. When Sarah compares him to his brother, Hannibal sings a freedom hymn:

> For the old man is a—waitin'
>
> For to carry you to freedom
>
> If you follow the Drinking Gourd.
>
> Follow–follow–follow . . .
>
> If you follow the Drinking Gourd . . . (174)
>
> He adds:
>
> But don't you worry, little Sarah. I'll come back. (He smoothes her hair and comforts her) I'll come back and buy you. Mama too, if she's still livin.' (176)

The Drinking Gourd is a powerful comment on the way people are treated as commodities to be bought and sold. Black slaves are threatened and prohibited to read or write. There are the harshest laws made in the slave code to keep them from being educated. The penalties for becoming educated are maiming, mutilation or death. Usually, this punishment is not only for those who attain education but also for the ones who might dare to teach, even white men. The fact of blinding the black hero named Hannibal is horrible enough. Anne Cheney observes:

> [I]nstitutions, unlike the individuals in them–are evil and all consuming. Also, Hannibal's experience demonstrates clearly that the white man's power to enslave the black man has as its foundation "the denial of literacy." His penalty for learning how to read, . . . "becomes both a literal and symbolic punishment. (qtd. in Lecson 73)

When Rissa comes to know that her son can read the Bible, she is very pleased. But later when she recalls how once both a black man who learned to read and a white man who taught him, were punished brutally by the Whites for this crime, Rissa tells her son to quit because she was horrified by the memory of that menacing incident and she did not want Hannibal to be the victim of the same.

There is a scene in act 2 of *The Drinking Gourd*, which Lorraine Hansberry has created very poignantly. This is a touching scene when little Hannibal is brutally punished:

> EVERET: You have used your master's son to commit a crime against your master. How long has this been going on? Who else have you taught, boy?. . . . There is only one thing I have ever heard of that was proper for an educated slave. It is like anything else; when a part is corrupted by disease. . . . When a part is corrupted by disease— one cuts out the disease. The ability to read in a slave is a disease. (209-10)

Hannibal was mercilessly blinded to deprive him of reading or writing. All this indicates that if Blacks even tried to challenge the white authority, their safety might be threatened by violent attacks. Whites believed that if slaves get any kind of knowledge or education, it will prove dangerous to the system of slavery. Thus, education of the Blacks was always discouraged by the Whites.

Suzan-Lori Parks also showcases the similar issues of slavery and gives a deeper understanding of the issue by expressing it through the medium of songs. In the play, *Father Comes Home From The Wars*, in part 1, Parks creates a song out of the situation linking it to the hopes and fears regarding getting freedom as Colonel, the master had promised Hero freedom for his services. The Colonel apologizes for assaulting Hero for no reasons and says, "A toast to you. . . . Honest, trustworthy. . . . taught me what little song I manage. . . .I am, actually singing your praises. Sing with me? The one about toiling?" (80). And then Colonel begins singing and the Hero, the slave joins in:

> Hero: In the darkest of the darkest night
>
> There is still a day that will come all right
>
> God is in his Heaven up above up above
>
> While we toil bravely down below. (81)

Suzan-Lori Parks has very well exemplified slavery in *The Death of the Last Man in the Whole Entire World* where she throws light on the predicament of Blacks who were separated from their families and were enslaved, exploited and sometimes even lynched. In the play, the Black Man wishes to free himself from the shackles of slavery. He begs for his freedom, "Will somebody take these straps of uh me please? I would like to use my hands" (110). He is in a state of bewilderment and frustration because of the fact that it is beyond his reach to come out of this trap of enslavement and he finds it impossible to do anything for himself and his people. He pleads for his freedom not only from the Whites but also from history that misrepresents him as he loses control over his own representation. Parks here uncovers two aspects of the word 'death.' Firstly, it points to lynching of African Americans and secondly it symbolizes the wide erasure of African American history from the recorded American history and culture so that Blacks can never be remembered, thus removing the traces of Blacks' existence from the history forever.

Parks mirrors the horror of lynching in her plays and the most literal manifestation of a lynching is rendered in the play, *The Death of the Last Black Man in the Whole Entire World,* where the protagonist, the Black Man appears on stage with a rope around his neck and Black Woman with Fried Drumstick responds, "let me loosen your collar for you comed home after uh hard days work… such uh hard days work that now you cant breathe you. Now" (118). Black Man in the play represents all dead black people who are tormented and lynched by the white society and speaks about the violence and oppression they have to endure—hanging, jettisoning and lynching.

The play powerfully refers to the era of slavery. It reveals that the atrocities of the past persist even now. Through Black Man's repeated deaths, Parks reveals the violent assaults that Blacks endured during slavery. Black Woman also talks about the fixity and stagnation in the lives of the Blacks. She says that nothing has changed in many years, "Today you sit in your chair you sat yesterday . . . day afore yesterday afore they come . . . tooked you. Things today is just as they are yesterday cept nothing is familiar cause it was such uh long time" (107).

Parks further depicts the period when slavery was abolished but Blacks were still engaged in subservient jobs. The play portrays the harsh treatment of slaves through the character Arthea, the newly emancipated slave in *Imperceptible Mutabilities,* in part 3, subtitled as "Open House." In the play, Arthea bids goodbye to the white family whom she had served almost throughout her life. The two children namely Anglor and Blanca treat her in an indifferent and disrespectful manner which is evident in their conversation with her:

ANGLOR: Today is her last day. She's gone slack.

BLANCA: Is today your last day, Arthea?. . . .

ANGLOR : You have to answer her.

BLANCA: You have to answer me.

ARTHEA: Yes, Missy. Mm goin. Mm goinuhway. . . .

ANGLOR: To do what?

ARTHEA: Dunno. . . . Goin uhwaytuh live, I guess. . .

ANGLOR: Who's going to clean their commodes?!

Who's going to clean our commodes?! We won't be

visit you because we won't be changed! (41-42)

Neither of the children shows any regard or affection for Arthea. They are just bothered about their personal needs that Arthea took care of as a slave.

Parks' play *Father Comes Home From The Wars* also deals with the issue of slavery. It unfolds the saga of an enslaved African American seeking his liberty from his white master. Hero is a slave on a plantation in West Texas. In part 1, "A Measure of a Man," Hero faces a great dilemma whether he should accompany his master to the war in Texas or not. His father advises him to go but his wife pleads with him to stay back. One of the characters, Homer says that he has actually no choice and will be a loser both ways. He says:

Homer: Ain't no game, Hero.

Cause you shouldn't be doing neither . . .

Cause both choices, Hero

To stay here and work the field

To go there and fight in the field

Both choices are

Nothing more than the same coin . . .

Two sides of the same coin

And the coin aint even in our pocket. (42)

Hero eventually makes a deal with his white master and decides to fight alongside his master in the Civil War. In return his master promises him freedom from slavery. Hero agrees to do the worst thing in order to get the best thing that is his freedom.

His betrayal of his friend Homer who tried to escape depicts his desperation to be set free. There is a cruel irony in the situation. His act is consequent upon the promise of freedom for cutting off his friend's foot, who was caught trying to escape:

Homer: Back then when I run off

We were supposed to head out together . . .

Boss-Master and his like finding me,

Surrounding me . . . And you cutting off my foot.

Hero: He threatened me with death . . . .

Homer: So after what he made you do to me.

How can you ever believe Boss-Master

When he promises you moon and stars?

Hero: Cause I ain't like you.

I ain't some wild man who will . . .

Go running. Go running here go running there. . . .

Grabbing, taking, snatching, begging, borrowing, stealing?

My Freedom's gonna be free of that.

Homer: Seems like

After all the wrong Boss has done

You're no better than a dog.

Or worse than a dog. (46)

Though, Hero was promised freedom many times, the promises always remain unfulfilled. But Hero still cherishes hope for a better future.

In the part 2, "A Battle in the Wilderness," Hero serves his master the Colonel, and his every task which also includes looking after Smith, a wounded white captain in the First Kansas colored Infantry, who was captivated by Colonel. Smith never wishes to own a slave but Colonel insists him to do so and offers him to buy Hero. It exemplifies the treatment of Blacks as a commodity or a property to be sold and used. Colonel asks Smith to guess Hero's purchase and promises to give him the possession of Hero forever if he guesses it right. Here, Hero's consent doesn't matter at all:

> Colonel: . . . . Before the sale was made, a prospective buyer would need to hear a report of your conduct. Hero's a good worker . . . he don't run off . . . To sum up the report of his conduct, we'll say, Hero minds his Master. That adds an extra hundred or two. . . . then we would be at a price of around 650. (73)

When Colonel asks Smith to inspect Hero to know his value, Hero resists but Colonel assaults him brutally, which brings to the forefront the harsh treatment of slaves:

> Colonel: Stand up Hero and undo yourself. We need to finish the inspection. (*Hero is thinking: Nope*)
>
> Colonel: Undo yourself.
>
> First, we will do a visual inspection and then, we'll do more than just look.
>
> Undo yourself, Hero.
>
> Hero: (*Hero is thinking: No fucking way*.)
>
> Smith: Stop.
>
> Colonel: Undo yourself I said.
>
> Smith: Stop.
>
> Colonel : Alright. For his sake. We wouldn't want the Yankee to die of fright. (The Colonel approaches Hero and, quickly raising his riding crop, he strikes Hero across the face). (79-80)

Parks illustrates through this scene, master's brutal treatment and her protagonist's struggle for freedom. Hero is tolerating all this just to get back his freedom. For majority of Black Americans, the question of what it means to be free in America is yet to be resolved. In second act of the play, Hero asks Smith that who will he belong to if he wins his freedom? He further says when someone will ask, "Whose nigger are you, Nigger?, I'm gonna say, "I belong to myself" ? Today I can say, 'I belong to the Colonel'" (96). At the outset only, Parks characterizes her narratives as evidence of subservience of Blacks under the Whites who define them from their frame of reference to emphasize how Blacks are owned by the master class.

In addition to focusing upon the manifold implications of slavery, Lorraine Hansberry also underscores segregation which is another pertinent issue associated with racism. On one hand black activists were trying hard to mark an end to segregation and on the other, black authors too were attempting to address these crucial issues through their writings. In *A Raisin in the Sun*, the issue of segregation is clearly visible which acquaints us with the stark racism that prevailed in 1950s in the United States of America. The events in the play are loosely based on an anti-segregation case that was won by Carl Hansberry in the Illinois Supreme Court. Hansberry has depicted in this play how segregation had become a social problem in America of the 1950s which separated the people of the same country on the basis of the colour of their skin. The play is set in the turbulent times of segregation, oppression and the Civil Rights Movement.

The play emphasizes that the Blacks need to put in a lot more effort to receive an equal treatment, or else they would be forced to be confined with, or satisfied with, their ghetto existence. The Whites never give them a chance to move ahead of them. Although, Hansberry family could afford good private schools, she was sent to the segregated public schools as her family worked in order to change the laws governing segregation. Chicago's discriminatory real estate covenants were in a way challenged by Hansberry's father by moving his family to Hyde Park which was all-white Chicago neighbourhood. Hansberry's encounter with racism in her white neighbourhood was quite brutal and violent. Due to an ingrained racism and violence perpetrated by the Whites, Hansberry's father was on the verge of taking his family to Mexico to live at the time of his death. Obviously, Blacks did not enjoy the liberty to buy houses of their own choice and to choose their neighbourhood according to their wishes.

This is borne out when Lena Younger wants her family to shift to a house which she bought with the insurance money that she got after her husband's death. This house is located in white people's colony. Lindner, a representative of white community, leaves no stone unturned to dissuade them from buying a house in white neighbourhood. However, he does not succeed in doing so. The following conversation reflects the fear of shifting to a white colony:

> MAMA: Well–well–it's out there in Clybourne Park—
>
> . . . .
>
> RUTH: Clybourne Park? Mama, there ain't no colored people living in Clybourne Park.
>
> MAMA: Well, I guess there's going to be some now.
>
> WALTER: (*Bitterly*) So that's the peace and comfort you went out and bought for us today. (93)

The play also throws light on the hypocrisy of the racist white society. This is reflected through the character of Karl Lindner. Although all the time he talks about brotherhood, his main purpose is to discourage the Younger family from buying a house in a white locality. Lindner explains that he represents the Clybourne Park Improvement Association which, among other things, welcomes new people, like the Youngers, to their community and also handles "special community problems." Beneatha senses what his mission is. As he proceeds to say that it is best to talk things out, and that race prejudice has nothing to do with it, he gradually works up to the point that his neighbourhood is for the Whites only. He says that the Association is willing to buy the house back from them for more than they paid. There is an undertone of threat in Lindner's talk when he has the first meeting with the Younger family. He says, "I am sure you people must be aware of some of the incidents which have happened in various parts of the city when colored people have moved into certain areas" (116).

Later when Walter refuses Karl Lindner's offer, Lindner's words seem to be more of a threat: "Well—if you are that final about it . . . there is nothing left for me to say. I sure hope you people know what you're getting into" (149).

Lorraine Hansberry depicts the extent of torture and hostility perpetrated on the Blacks by the Whites. She describes how Lena Younger's neighbour Mrs. Johnson expresses her happiness at their good fortune but at the same time she talks about a newspaper report about how Whites had bombed a black family. She goes to the extent of saying that the Younger family might be the next to be named in the paper for the same reason. Hansberry, thus, reveals the harsh truth of differential treatment meted out to the Blacks, forcing them to live in constant fear.

Communal Unity

Hansberry and Parks write for the entire community and nation by focusing on reinforcing communal unity, racial bonding and cultural oneness which racism tends to shatter by the divide and rule policy. Both the playwrights foreground the theme of quest for unity among Blacks in their respective works. They track in their plays the experiences of African Americans' memory of racism and poverty to reclaim a sense of selfhood and communal identity as well as unity. While demonstrating the significance of the past and black heritage in the formation of identity of Blacks, both the playwrights put forth their viewpoint that Blacks' awareness of their worth, glorifying African culture and values can help them salvage their identity. They suggest that Blacks should assert for their rights by coming together instead of suffering and surrendering to the wishes of the dominant community.

Parks exemplifies through her works that the traumatic memory of Blacks from slave ships to the violence perpetrated on them is vital to reclaim their individual as well as communal identity. The black experience and history were erased by the hegemonic white colonial system. Parks attempts to recreate the past through postcolonial perspective and rewrites the history by including the truth of black community in it, which was ignored in past. This way, she manages to restore the blackness in history. The characters in her plays do not represent only themselves but the whole black community. Their shared traumatic past gives them a sense of belonging.

Emphasizing the community bonding, Parks emphasizes on doing away with the gender disparity in her plays. She emphasizes that in order to eradicate racial oppression; the unity of the black community is indispensable. In her play, *The Death of the Last Black man in the Whole Entire World,* a bond of solidarity among black men and women is exemplified through the relationship between the Black Man with the Watermelon and the Black Woman with the Fried Drumstick. Parks represents this mythical black couple who stand by each other against all odds and crises of life. Even after the trauma of his multiple deaths, associated with the oppressions of Blacks, the Black Man always comes back home because he knows that his woman is waiting and cares for him. At one point of time, Black Man is not able to move his hands symbolizing loss of his strength but Black Woman comforts him by becoming his strength. It is her courage that leads Black

Man to survive continuously even as he suffers multiple violent deaths.

In *Father Comes Home from the Wars*, when Smith reveals to Hero that he's actually a Black man and a former slave, Hero immediately releases him from the cage. The following conversation between the two illustrates the sense of oneness and brotherhood among them:

> Smith: It was my Captain who died. On the battlefield . . . I put his coat on over mine to keep warm.
>
> Hero: You're a Private serving in the 1st Kansas Colored Infantry.
>
> Smith: That's right.
>
> Hero: The 1st Kansas Coloreds they got Coloreds as Privates.
>
> Smith: That's right.
>
> Hero: You a Coloredman?. . . .
>
> Hero: You think you all will beat the Jebs?
>
> Smith: God willing. And then the whole world will change. You will be able to have your own farm. Or you'll move North. . . . (94)

Later he unties the rope from Smith's neck, going against his Master Colonel's command. He risks his own life to release his black brother:

> Hero: I don't know if I'm qualified to give freedom to another man seeing as how I'm not a free man myself but I give it to you just the same. . . .

Hero: No matter. If you're lucky you could move down the hill some, lay low for a spell, then join back up with your fellahs.

Smith: How you gonna explain me being gone?

Hero: I'll think of something. Not to worry. (101-02)

His act of freeing Smith from the clutches of his master depicts a Black's concern and affection for another Black. Though Smith keeps on asking Hero to join in, he himself stays and heads southward, taking the path Colonel took, back towards the heart of the Rebel Army.

Lorraine Hansberry also showcases cohesion within the family as a source of strength in both the plays. *A Raisin in the Sun* and *The Drinking Gourd*, signal the possibility of cooperation between the African Americans owing to the sustenance they draw from each other within their family, which in a way reflects a profound understanding of how a family is spiritually cemented. The three generations of the Younger family have contrasting dreams, speech, religious and musical preferences, which reflect the richness and diversity of black culture. Each family member has different dreams and aspirations but they unite together to fulfil the dream of buying a house which will lead to the happiness of the entire family. Lorraine portrays the importance of communal unity in general and importance of family in particular through the members of Younger family, who sacrifice their dreams for the sake of each other and overcome adversity together. In *The Drinking Gourd* also, Hansberry highlights the bonding between the mother and the son when Rissa, who had always been an obedient slave to her master leaves her dying master for the sake of her son who is mutilated by the master's son. She takes the gun of her master and bids farewell to Sarah, Hannibal and her grandson Joshua to run away to the North for freedom.

In her autobiographical play, *To Be Young Gifted and Black*, Hansberry says:

> What we are interested in is making perfectly clear that between the Negro intelligentsia, the Negro middle class, and the Negro this-and-that –we are one people. And that as far as we are concerned, we are represented by the Negroes in the streets of Birmingham! (229)

This bears out the importance of communal unity to fight against the white dominance. By referring to such instances, both the writers highlight the spirit of oneness among Blacks during the times of colonial era.

Dichotomy of the American Dream: Myth or Reality

The American dream is an ideology that is a source of inspiration and at the same time bitterness. Some people realized this but it became a nightmare for many. On the face of it, the American Dream promises freedom, equality, economic stability, however in reality, it remains a distant fantasy to be achieved. Lorraine Hansberry and Suzan-Lori Parks share a definite and identical vision about the American Dream. They have highlighted both the aspects—the aspirations, dreams and hopes of the black people and on the other the frustration, alienation and confusion peculiar to their lives. The American Dream remains an illusion for Blacks but they were fascinated by it.

Lorraine Hansberry's plays cover numerous aspects related to the dreams and aspirations of the black people. The title of the play, *A Raisin in the Sun* is taken from Langston Hughes's poem "Harlem" which is suggestive of explosive quality of the dreams nurtured by the Younger family—Walter, Mama, Ruth and Beneatha. The poem reflects the frustration and despair of the American Negro, an energy which can be turned into violence and self-destruction if not fulfilled.

In the play, all the four members of the family have their own dreams—dreams which are waiting to be fulfilled. The Youngers, a lower-class black family living in Chicago desire to gain middle-class acceptance. The play follows their struggles and frustrations in pursuit of the American Dream. The inability to fulfil their dreams brings desolation and frustration to them. Being Blacks, they have to make greater efforts to achieve their dreams. This poignantly brings to the fore the racial inequality in America. The Younger family's aspiration is to move out of the ghetto at all costs. In act 1, scene 1, Lena younger tells Ruth about her and Big Walter's dreams:

> MAMA: I remember just as well the day me and Big Walter moved in here. Hadn't been married but two weeks and wasn't planning on living here no more than a year. We was going to set away little by little, don't you know, and buy a little place out in Morgan Park. We had even picked out the house. Looks right dumpy today. But Lord, child, you should know all the dreams I had 'bout buying that house and fixing it up and making me a little garden in the back—And didn't none of it happen. (45)

She adds:

> Big Walter used to say, he'd get right wet in the eyes sometimes, lean his head back with the water standing in his eyes and say, "Seem like God didn't see fit to give the black man nothing but dreams–but he did give us children

> to make them dreams seem worthwhile." (*She smiles*) He could talk like that, don't you know. (46)

These conversations bear out the helplessness and unrealized dreams of the Blacks who found it difficult to enjoy equal opportunities. Each of the main characters cherishes a dream, hoping to improve the family's situation. It has been Lena Younger's dream to escape the "rat trap" of the ghetto, while her grandson thinks it a sport to watch the killing of a rat. Big Walter has also a big dream to buy a house but even after his death due to overwork, his dream is not fulfilled. Walter and Beneatha, who are siblings, have dreams of rising above their present socioeconomic status. Beneatha wants to be a doctor because of her desire to cure her people. And Walter Lee wants to be a rich man and wants to enter business by becoming a partner in a liquor store because according to him only money can raise his status. Walter Lee is a man who is furious and frustrated with his current position in life because he feels that being a man of the family, he is a big failure. He works as a chauffeur for a white man, a job that brings him no contentment. His dissatisfaction is reflected when he speaks to his wife Ruth and says, "I'm thirty-five years old; I've been married eleven years and I got a little boy who sleeps in the living room and all I got to give him is stories about how rich white people live" (34).

Malcolm Johnson observes, "Hansberry's *A Raisin in the Sun* continues to be relevant because, still, for most of black America, the dream is still deferred, the chemistry for explosion is still at flashpoint" (qtd. in Leeson 101). The dreams that Big Walter's family has about the insurance money represent black America's dreams that have been suppressed by the white oppressors. The money is not enough to fulfil all the dreams and the rift between the family arises. Beneatha's African suitor Asagai also dreams of returning home to Africa. Proud of his African heritage, he believes that one can only be contented in the place one belongs to. Africans belong to Africa so they will never feel comfortable anywhere else. He dreams of transforming the social as well as the political landscape in Africa to make it a better place to live in for his people.

Through each of the characters, Hansberry depicts how the dreams of black America have been modified or deferred. Initially the characters' dreams are confined to fulfilling their small wishes through the insurance money, but by the end of the play, to protect the dignity of the family becomes more important to them than money. It is revealed in the play that due to the curse of racism and economic oppression, it becomes difficult or even impossible to attain the American dream. At the same time, however, the play depicts the hopeful joviality of the black American family.

Similarly, Parks portrays in her plays as to how Blacks' dreams and aspirations for attaining equality and financial security remain a dream only and changes into a frustration with the passage of time. Blacks are confined only to financial and occupational limits. Parks challenges the notion of the American Dream in her Pulitzer-Prize winning play, *Topdog/Underdog*. The fallacy of the American Dream exists as a salient theme in the play. She portrays the living condition of two brothers Lincoln and Booth who fail to cash in on their aspiration to realize the American dream exposing the fallacy of the American Dream. The two brothers struggle throughout to raise their social and economic level to get recognition in the American society. Booth practices skills in three-card game to make money and Lincoln works in an arcade as an Abraham Lincoln impersonator. Booth dreams of earning fortune on streets whereas Lincoln dreams of retaining his job to sustain his livelihood but unfortunately despite all the efforts made by Booth and Lincoln, they fail in the pursuit of happiness and success in their lives as Booth ultimately discovers that he will never be able to master the card game due to lack of training and Lincoln loses his job as an outcome of a technical advancement as he realizes that a wax dummy can easily replace an impersonator. Parks also points to the Reverend Martin Luther King's dream which is yet to be realized by alluding to; "I have a dream" speech that placed the struggle of the Blacks in a historical context. He says, "he had a dream that "the sons of forever slaves and the sons of former slave owners will be able to sit down together at the table of brotherhood" (Kachur 12). Referring to these lines Larson says:

> By evoking the words of Martin Luther King Jr., the play makes Lincoln's struggle timeless and equates his struggle with the Lincoln costume to a struggle for civil rights and personal freedom. But as in King's speech, these rights and freedoms, at least for Lincoln and Booth, are still just a dream. The brothers are bound by all the costume signifies: revisionist history, slavery, racism, double-consciousness, poverty, and even their own personalities. (74)

At the end of the play, when both the brothers are unable to get rid of their woeful life, Parks highlights the illusory nature of the American Dream. The failure in achieving their goals and living their dreams, Lincoln and Booth end up destroying each other. Booth's frustration and aggression rises and Lincoln, after losing his job, gets back to the card game which he had been avoiding since long. When Lincoln suggests Booth to seek an employment for himself and to keep Grace with him, Booth gets offended and challenges him to a game of Three Card Monte. Lincoln asks Booth to wager on the game $500, an inheritance which his mother gave him on the day she left. He has not touched it since he was eleven and has kept in the stockings. For Booth, this inheritance is his support and back up. And when Lincoln wins and attempts to take away the inheritance money which symbolizes Booth's familial memories, Booth threatens him but Lincoln continues to tease him and takes a knife to open the stockings which hold the money. Eventually Booth loses his temper:

> Booth: Only so long I can stand that little brother shit. Can only take it so long. Im telling you—
>
> LINCOLN: Take it back, man. . . .
>
> BOOTH: Who thuh man now, huh?. . . . Aint laughing at me you was just laughing bunch uh bullshit and you know it.
>
> LINCOLN: Here, Take it.
>
> BOOTH: I aint gonna be needing it. Go on. You won it you open it. . . .
>
> You stole my inheritance, man. . . . Ima take back my inheritance too. . . .
>
> She didn't give it to you. And I been saving it all this while. (112-14)

He was no longer in a state to deal with his sense of sibling inferiority and in rage he shoots Lincoln in order to get back his money and his link to his mother. Thus, Parks subtly reveals the illusionary aspect of the American Dream for Blacks as the idea of it has given both the brothers a ray of hope to overcome their poverty and thus raise their social status in the society. This does not work in their favour at all and worsens their situation.

Phenomenology of Black Identity and Pride

Ziauddin Sardar says:

> *Black Skin, White Masks* offer a very particular definition of dignity. Dignity is not located in seeking equality with the white man and his civilization... It is about being oneself with all the multiplicities, system and contradictions of one's own ways of being, doing, knowing. It is about being true to oneself. . . . (vii)

African Americans were invisible, ghettoized and largely marginalized in everyday life. Lorraine Hansberry and Suzan-Lori Parks address the issues of black dignity and identity in a passionate manner. Hansberry's *A Raisin in the Sun* and *The Drinking Gourd* powerfully deal with these issues. She emphasizes that though Blacks serve the Whites, their dignity and honour is always precious to them. In act 1, scene 2 of *A Raisin in the Sun*, when Lena Younger speaks to her son Walter Lee, it is clear that the older generations valued dignity and freedom over money even in most unfavourable circumstances:

> MAMA: Son- how come you talk so much about money?
>
> WALTER: (*With immense passion*) Because it is life Mama!
>
> MAMA: Oh—(very quietly) Oh—(*very quietly*) So now it's life. Money is life. Once upon a time freedom used to be life—now its money. I guess the world really do change . . .

> WALTER: No–it was always money . . . We just didn't know about it.
>
> MAMA: No . . . something has changed. (*She looks at him*) You something new, boy. In my time we was worried about not being lynched and getting to the North if we could and how to stay alive and still have a pinch of dignity too . . . (74)

According to Alvarez, "Although *A Raisin in the sun* is occasionally "trite," it makes for an extraordinary compelling evening's theatre. Hansberry uses powerful rhetoric to explore such issues as natural dignity" (qtd. in Leeson 100). In act 3, Walter asserts that his honour is his most valued possession by refusing the offer of Lindner, a representative of the Clybourne Park Improvement Association. Walter tells Lindner that the Youngers come from generations of proud people. He adds:

> And we have decided to move into our house because my father—my father—he earned it for us brick by brick. We don't want to make no trouble for nobody or fight no causes, and we will try to be good neighbors. And that's all we got to say about that. We don't want your money. (148)

Big Walter is represented as a symbol of pride and is seen by all as a role model of the family. At the close of act I, Lena tells her son that he has to be the man his father was. It is revealed that the Younger family is a family with a lot of pride and dignity, who struggle and seek hope to better their position in this corrupt society. Thomas P. Alder observes, "*A Raisin in the Sun* examines the ethic that equates 'being somebody' with material success while urging a new generation of black men to achieve dignity by coming into their own as husbands and fathers" (qtd. in Leeson 50).

The African ceremonial dance also invokes racial pride and feeling of oneness between Walter and Beneatha. While experiencing racial pride, Walter attempts to revive his lost African past and says, "OH, DO YOU HEAR, MY BLACK BROTHERS! . . . Telling us to prepare for the GREATNESS OF THE TIME!" (79). Margaret B. Wilkerson rightly says:

> Walter, therefore, can be seen as signaling the wave of the future. He is restless, hungry, angry—a victim of his circumstance but at the same time the descendant of his proud forebears, struggling to transcend his victimhood. (qtd. in Bloom 35)

The same theme pervades *The Drinking Gourd* too where Hannibal, a young a nineteen year old boy believes that the only good slave is a bad slave. He tries his best to keep his human dignity, even if his manner may appear too weird. He breaks tools; works slowly, plays sick and often disappears for hours at a time. When his mother Rissa counsels him to do his work and tells him to be thankful to have such a benevolent master as Hiram Sweet, Hannibal says that he plans to become a bad slave, pretend to be stupid instead of smart, be lazy instead of quick and sick instead of healthy. He thinks the more pain his behaviour gives to his master; the more Hannibal is a man. Hannibal wishes to go to the North in search of liberty and identity to follow his brother in his quest to regain dignity and freedom for black slaves.

Suzan-Lori Parks also emphasizes that race and ethnicity are vital to the understanding of Blacks' identity in history. Her plays throw light on black people's suffering in order to bring to forefront the everyday experience of African Americans:

> Parks has produced provocative dramas that capture the nightmares of African Americans endangered by a white establishment determined to erase their history and eradicate their dreams. . . . Her disarming sets and dislocating narratives deconstruct a linear, ordered sense of history . . . Her characters are displaced versions of themselves, trying to find their identity–in a family, a city, a nation, a continent, the universe. (Kolin 1)

The very title of the play *Imperceptible Mutabilities in The Third Kingdom* places emphasis on the mutation of Blacks. Parks alludes to the Middle Passage and the third space which Bhabha terms as "interruptive, interrogative, and enunciative" (qtd. in Russell 3). Through the reference to the five seers in part 3 "Third Kingdom," Parks portrays the dilemma faced by the Blacks vis-à-vis their existence. In the beginning, all the five seers speak and repeat their names: Kin Seer, Us-Seer, Shark-Seer, Soul-Seer and Over-Seer depicting their urge for a stable identity which is presently in a fragmented form. The seers dream of jumping off the ship and then swimming to the shore. This can be connected with the Africans hurled overboard during Middle Passage. The isolation, dismemberment and alienation experienced by the Blacks is powerfully conveyed here. Particularly through the character Kin-Seer, Parks communicates the slaves' parlous passage across the Atlantic and describes the divided self of Blacks as Kin-Seer does not recognize himself until Over-Seer—the representative of the white world assures him of his identity. *In Souls of Black Folk*, Du Bois writes:

> African Americans are born with a veil, and gifted with second-sight in this American world,—a world which yields him no true self-consciousness, but only lets him see himself through the revelation of the other world . . . this sense of always looking at one's self through the eyes of others . . . One ever feels his two-ness,—an American, a Negro; two souls, two thoughts, two reconciled strivings; two warring ideals in one dark body, whose dogged strength alone keeps it from being torn asunder. (qtd. in Larson 10-11)

Parks showcases the plight of her characters, lost in a white world resulting in erasure of their true identities. Though they recognize their captivity and impoverished selfhood, they consistently search for their identity as well as a justification for their existence. They represent different eras and groups but all of them often face identity crisis. They are always in conflict with their actual selves and the imposed identities. The player tries to describe his dream in which he was standing in the dirt and there was nothing in front of him except water. He was waving and waving at his other self who could barely see him. All this drives home the idea of a divided self as an aftermath of slavery which haunts him. One of the characters namely Kin –Seer says, "Last night I dreamed of where I comed from. But where I comed from diduhnt look like nowhere like I been" (37). Here he articulates his dream of the place where he came from and the place where he is right now which is alien to him. The conversation illuminates the concept of otherness and the fear of losing identity.

He prompts Over-seer to look back for his lost self and says, "You said I could wave as long as I see um. I still see un" (40). All this refers to the period when they were taken far away from their home across the Middle Passage on the slave ship when they lost their identities as well as dignity. Shark-Seer articulates his own dreamscape and articulates the similar loss of identity and says:

> I dream up uh fish that swalloin me and I dream up uh me that is then becamin that fish and uh dream of that fish becamin uh shark and I dream of that shark becamin uh shore . . . And I whuduhnt me no more and I whudunht no fish. My new self was uh third Self madethuh space in between. (39)

The play, thus, showcases a sense of extreme alienation of the slaves. The Third-self signifies losing their true self due to being trapped into the world of slavery, being deported far away from their homeland to an alien place. Parks suggests clearly in her essay, "An Equation for Black People Onstage" that the African Americans need to have their own identities, as individuals rather than in relationship to the Whites.

When Suzan-Lori Parks started writing, it was quite difficult to change or reform mindsets but she paved the way for the Blacks to create a separate identity for themselves other than that associated with blackness and oppression. She endeavours to reinstate the historical facts and events pertaining to black suffering in order to highlight the predicament of the African Americans. The Black Man in *The Death of the Last Black Man in the Whole Entire World* is unable to understand the connection between his name and appearance. He asks his wife, 'Was me green and stripedly when we first comed out?" (107). He is forced to represent himself over and over again with the folk stereotype associated with Blacks. It is further underlined that the name watermelon embodies the oppression and slavery exposing the historical truth about Blacks who remain confined to peculiar identities assigned to them while their actual identities remain hidden. The characters in the play are authentic representation of the African Americans. The protagonist is seen questioning his identity as well as his existence:

> Today's African Americans must deal with the traumatic memory of slavery and the repetition of cycles of violence and poverty in order to reclaim a sense of individual personhood and communal identity. (Wetmore Jr. and Howard 74)

Racial stereotypes hinder Blacks to express themselves and their identity and thus hamper them to create their space in white dominated world.

In Parks' other plays, *The America Play* and *Topdog/Underdog*, we see the main characters impersonating Lincoln, the president of America. Coincidentally both the characters have the same name as well, that is Lincoln. They often talk about their costumes which in a way hide their black identity and associate them with the white identity in terms of their clothing. The makeup and the masks cover the actors' identity wholly. "Their performance underlines the cruel deceptions/illusions the white world forces on African Americans. Watching shows in Parks, then, as in Kennedy, is essential to identity (de)construction" (Kolin 15). "For Foundling Father and Lincoln, the costume's effect is internal; it distracts and disrupts their perceptions of their true interior selves"(Larson 60). Lincoln in *Topdog/Underdog* says, "They say the clothes make the man. All day long I wear that getup. But that don't make me who I am"(33). He emphasizes that there is a difference between his job and his real self and asserts that he does not like to wear his costumes outside of work and believes in his own separate identity. He adds that his job will never decide who he really is. But contrary to that, The Foundling Father in *The America Play* identifies with Lincoln. He explains that he has got the opportunity to do the particular job just because he can perform Lincoln. He says, "While the Great Man's livelihood kept him in Big Town the Lesser Known work kept him in Small Town" (160). He adds:

> And when someone remarked that he played Lincoln so well that he ought to be shot, it was as if the Great Mans footsteps had been suddenly revealed. . . . The public was invited to pay a penny . . . enter the darened box and "SHOOT Mr. Lincoln." The Lesser Known became famous overnight. (164)

Lincoln in the play enacts the assassination of Lincoln, the President and costumers are invited to play the role of John Wilkes Booth to shoot him for a penny. He repeatedly performs this on the stage which symbolizes murder of a black man and his identity. In the play, The Foundling Father's comparison of himself with Lincoln throughout the play suggests the influence of whiteness and their culture on the newly emancipated African American slaves. He combats with his natural self and blackness by using white make up to hide his black skin. This act of impersonating Lincoln further gives a message that blackness is always conditional to whiteness. Throughout the play, an allusive move of digging for the Foundling Father's bones by his wife Lucy and his son, Brazil emphasizes the fact that the search is not for Lincoln's memory, but for the legacy of the Lesser Known, the black man whose identity was throughout overshadowed by the

Great Man's persona which is ultimately attained by the act of mimicry undertaken by the Lesser Known grave digger:

> Through his imitation of Lincoln, the Foundling Father begins to blur the boundaries between the original works sampled from the Greater Man . . . The Foundling Father tells us that he first began to construct his identity in relationship to "greatness" when he and Lucy took a trip to visit . . . After this trip, The Foundling Father realized that he was called to "greatness" : . . . the part he played in it all gave shape to the life and posterity of the Lesser Known that he could never shake. (Persley 73)

The Foundling Father has left his family to pursue his career as an impersonator of Lincoln. He was a gravedigger before he became an established impersonator. He feels embarrassed of his past vocation as a gravedigger and he calls himself as 'the Lesser known" instead. It is quite ironical that a black man while hiding his own black identity has to perform wearing a whiteface, the death of a public figure, who stood for the African-Americans. In digging, Foundling Father's family search for a heritage, which can provide them with a sense of historical continuity and recognition. Brazil does not follow in his father's footsteps even as his mother Lucy believes and tells him that there is nothing to be ashamed of being a gravedigger. Brazil, digs and searches for the evidence of his father's existence:

> LUCY: . . . Dig on, son—Cant stop diggin till you dig up something . . . Its own place. Along with thuh other discoveries . . .
>
> BRAZIL: Uh huhn. . . .
>
> Ff Pa was here weud find his bones. (177)

Parks digs into the past to recover and reconstruct the narratives that had been erased from the history. She finds it necessary to bring back the black history by representing the traditional events and figures.

In the play, *Topdog/Underdog* Parks deals with the pretence of everyday life and at the same time with the performative aspects of life:

> The metaphor of 'performance' as a way of describing the way the identities are produced and maintained has a varied and complex genealogy. Concepts like Du Bois's double-consciousness', Bakhtin's 'heteroglossia' . . . all contribute to an understanding that cultural, gendered, and racial identities work in relation to shared discourses which act like script's for an individual's performance of a particular identity. (Wetmore Jr and Howard 75)

In *Topdog/Underdog* both the brothers attempt to define the 'other' and establish an identity of a patriarchal income producer and head of the family. In order to gain a foothold in the American society, they assert themselves as patriarchs. Parks depicts both sides of the cool pose: performative as well as destructive. This cool pose is used by Booth and Lincoln, to hide their frustration and disappointments in life and to counter societal pressure. They try to build their identities in order to supersede each other. "The 'topdog' needs the underdog to continually define and redefine his dominance" (Wetmore Jr and Howard 76). Though they are deprived in terms of economic comfort, still they assert themselves as patriarchs as Walter does in *A Raisin in the Sun*, boasting of himself as the only male member in the family. Richard Wright rightly contends:

> African-Americans historically had to engage in a kind of 'black acting' in order to survive within Euro-dominated society, a process called 'masking' that Richard Majors and Janet Mancini-Billson explore in *Cool Pose: The Dilemmas of Black Manhood America*. 'Cool pose' is a performative identity adopted by African-American males. Some African-American males have channeled their creative energies into the construction of symbolic universe. Denied access to mainstream avenues of success, they have created their own voice. Unique patterns of speech, work and demeanor express the cool pose. (qtd. in Howard 102-03)

In *Topdog/Underdog*, in the first scene, Booth expresses his wish to change his name reclaiming ancestral origins. But Lincoln advises him not to do so as it will lead to minimizing of opportunities for him. He restrains Booth from adopting his actual identity. The following lines depict the acceptability/relevance of being "white" and rejection/ irrelevance of being black:

> LINCOLN: You gonna call yrself something African? . . . no one is gonna hire you if they cant say yr name. And some of the fellas who got they African names, no one can say they names and they cant say they names neither. I mean, you don't want yr new handle to obstruct yr employment possibilities. (18)

Booth was against his brother, Lincoln's work because he believes that it is detestable on black man's part to disguise himself as white just for the sake of money. Booth links Lincoln's plight to the domination of Blacks by Whites in the period of slavery: "Dressing up like some crackerass white man, some dead president and letting people shoot at You play Honest Abe. You aint going back but you going all the way back. Back to way back then when folks was slaves and shit" (27).

When Lincoln offers Booth to get the arcade to hire him, Booth refuses by saying, "That shit. ain't for me. I ain't into pretending I'm someone else all day . . . Least I'm still me!" (95). At one point of time when Lincoln loses his job as he is replaced by a wax dummy, he thinks of compromising with his employer regarding his salary and says, "I could tell him I'll take another pay cut. Thatll get him to take me back" (65). But hearing this Booth tries to convince him to be free and says, "Link. Yr free. Dont go crawling back. Yr free at last! Now you can do anything you want. Yr not tied down by that job. You can do something else. Something that pays better maybe" (65).

Reversing Stereotypical Blacks Images

Prolonged history of enslavement has led to creation of a negative self-image in the Blacks. Whites have persistently endorsed negative images about Blacks in order to deprive them of their own authentic selves and history. According to Mercer and Julen, "Racism defined African peoples as having only bodies and no minds: Black men and women were seen as muscle machines and thus the super exploitation of slavery could be justified" (qtd. in Davies 54).

Lorraine Hansberry raises question on the perpetuated stereotypes of the African Americans which lead to their social disintegration. Through her works, she challenges the world view regarding her people and counters the reality of racial discrimination and stereotypes associated with African Americans by immortalizing African culture and ethics. Stereotypical images about Africans that they have more than one wife suggesting that they are not civilized people are counteracted by Tshembe in *Les Blancs* through his response to Charlie:

> CHARLIE: You married?
>
> TSHEMBE: Yes. I have, however, only one wife!
>
> CHARLIE : Look, I thought we had decided to assume that the other was something more than an ass, Matoseh.
>
> TSHEMBE : It may be . . . that I had developed counter assumptions because I have had too much conversation in your country and in Europe. (73)

Parks also portrays African American experiences and challenges the racial and gendered stereotypes of African Americans by questioning their origins. She reclaims cultural identity by appropriation of these negative images that confine Blacks to be seen from Whites' perspective. Deliberately revisiting the misrepresentations of Blacks, Parks seeks to ascertain the real black identity. In *The Death of the Last Man in the Whole Entire World,* the lead characters Black Man with Watermelon and Black Woman with Fried Drumstick who represent the images of the folk plantation life, conjure up stereotypes and myths associated with blackness. The character named Black Man with Watermelon assures that watermelon does not belong to him, "This doesn't belong to me. Somebody planted this on me. On me in my hands" (105). This shows that deep inside, he has no connection with stereotypes associated with his identity by white hegemonic historiography. Blacks believe that Whites make it necessary for Blacks to present themselves in a stereotypical manner. As Black Man thinks that he must look like a melon from the melon patch. His sad plight of being entrapped in the worst part of African American history is depicted as he is reduced to only as an embodiment of a folk stereotype and is forced to live his life with that image. He asserts and re-defines his identity on his own by claiming that he sees himself in his own physical body. He explains, "I kin tell whats mine by whats got my looks. Ssmymethod . . . Look down at my foot and wonder it its mine. Foot mine? I kin as it and through uh looks like my looks thuh foot gives me back uh 'yes sir. Ssmymethod" (107). These words illustrate that due to oppression the black man is unsure of what really belongs to him. The black man exemplifies plight of all the black men who are tormented and rejected by the white society. The trauma of multiple deaths, lynching and the Middle Passage become a part of his identity as a black man.

Parks further reverses the stereotype of black man who mistreats his wife and family. In the play this Black Man respects the Black Woman in his life who cares for him. As bell hooks says, "The image of black masculinity that emerges from slave narratives is one of hardworking men who longed to assume full patriarchal responsibility for families and kin" (qtd in Wetmore Jr and Howard 51).

Parks, thus, emphatically interrogates the racist paradigms and negative portrayals of Blacks. Disrupting existing stereotypes of Blacks which devoid them of their actual identity, she endeavours to satirize the conventional racial representations by naming Blacks like Black Man with Watermelon, Black Woman with Fried Drumstick, Yes and Greens Black-Eyed Peas Cornbread, Lots of Grease and Lots of Pork, etc. Through a reference to the biblical story of Noah cursing his dark skinned son Ham, Parks exposes the history of racial inequality dating back to the time when historian Erik Seeman uncovered a story about an African American speaker who asserted his rights in the realm of colonial discourse. Greenwich, a Connecticut slave presented his viewpoint on slavery, symbolizing the self-assertion of Blacks' part. The biblical story of Noah's disrespectful son Ham is used by Whites to justify Blacks' enslavement and discrimination. Ham represents the collective memories and experiences of the African ancestors of African Americans. By referring to Ham, Parks exposes the still persisting historic fact of racial injustice and its justification by religious myth.

The role of media is always central in developing a strong image about something when it reaches out to people. In America, media has propagated negative images and hatred towards African Americans thus perpetuating racial prejudices representing them as destructive. In the play, *The Death of the Last Black Man in the Whole Entire World,* the news of Blacks' deaths is depicted as a thing of joy and celebrations, "News of Major's death sparked controlled displays of jubilation in all corners of the world" (110). Media has the power to reshape the attitude and perceptions of audiences which can be disparaging for the black identities.

Cultural Assimilation

Fanon asserts:

> Whiteness, has become a symbol of purity, of Justice, Truth, Virginity. It defines what it means to be civilized, modern and human. That is why the Negro knows nothing of the cost of freedom; when he has fought for Liberty and Justice . . . these were always white liberty and white justice that is values secreted by his masters. (qtd. in Sardar xiii)

Fanon wanted to alter the perspective that only whiteness symbolizes civilization and other positive aspects. He suggests that

Blacks are expected to consider their culture and history naïve and assimilate into white culture. However, voices of protest and urge for liberation could not be contained for long. The struggle to assert their identity began to define the black experience. "The struggle is concerned as much with freedom from colonialism as with liberation from the suffocating embrace of Europe, and the pretensions of its civilization to be the universal destiny of all humanity" (Sardar xii). Fanon considers this struggle as an effort for survival and a quest for liberty. He questions the colonial influence on native culture. In *Black Skin, White Masks*, he emphasizes the internalization of colonial culture and its consequent racist representation of the Blacks which leads to a self-division, self-hatred and alienation in the black subject. Ziauddin Sardar says:

> At first sight, Fanon is rather hard on the "black man." He is supposed to be a good nigger who even lacks the advantage of being able to accomplish this descent into a real hell. But Fanon's anger is directed not towards the "black man" but the proposition that he is required not only to be black but he must be black in relation to the white man. . . . He ceases to be a self-motivated person. The entire purpose of his behavior is to emulate the white man, to become like him, and thus hope to be accepted as a man. It is the dynamic of inferiority that concerns Fanon; and which ultimately he wishes to eliminate. (xiii)

Assimilation is considered as the process of adapting to the culture of a group. The theme of assimilation is a prominent theme in *A Raisin in the Sun*, which is depicted through the character of George Murchison, Beneatha's suitor, who manifests contempt for African roots and attempts to adopt American culture. He believes that he can achieve his goals only after abandoning his African heritage and adopting the western culture.

When Ruth asks Beneatha as to what it means to be an assimilationist? Beneatha answers her and says, "It means someone who is willing to give up his own culture and submerge himself completely in the dominant . . . oppressive culture" (81). To this George immediately replies: " . . . oh, dear dear . . . A lecture on the African past! On our Great West African Heritage! "Let's face it baby, your heritage is nothing but a bunch of raggedy-assed spirituals and some grass huts!" (81).

George Murchison engages in a heated debate with her when he sees her dancing with her brother in the traditional African costume. George has assimilated white culture which is reflected in his dress sense and the way he acts. He mocks Beneatha for wearing the African garb. Beneatha makes it very clear that she is not an assimilationist and that she would rather imbibe her own heritage than try to imitate white culture. Thus, Beneatha and George provide contrasting perspectives on assimilation.

Hansberry focuses on the idea of Africa as a home for African Americans and clearly illustrates it through her character, Joseph Asagai, a Nigerian student. Following the loss of Walter's investment Asagai tells a disheartened Beneatha: "come home with me. . . . across the ocean: home—to Africa. . . . Three hundred year later African Prince rose up out of the seas and swept the maiden back across the middle passage over which her ancestors had come—"(136). Asagai's suggestion to Beneatha to move to Nigeria with him to explore her African roots reflects his love and belief in black culture. After Joseph Asagai refers to Beneatha's straightened hair as "mutilated," Beneatha reevaluates the significance of her "assimilationist" hairstyle and decides to cut her hair and wear it in its natural form:

ASAGAI: . . . You wear it well . . . very well . . . mutilated hair and all.

BENEATHA :My hair—what's wrong with my hair?

ASAGAI *(shrugging):* Were you born with it like that?

BENEATHA: No . . . of course not.

ASAGAI *(smiling):* How then?

BENEATHA: You know perfectly well how . . . as crinkly as yours . . . that's how.

ASAGAI: And it is ugly to you that way?

BENEATHA :Oh, no—not ugly . . . But it's so hard to manage when it's, well—raw.

ASAGAI: And so to accommodate that—you mutilate it every week?

BENEATHA: It's not mutilation!

ASAGAI : . . . You came up to me and you said . . . I thought you were the most serious little thing I had ever seen—you said: "Mr.Asagai, I want very much to talk with you. About Africa . . . I am looking for my identity!"

BENEATHA *(turning to him, not laughing):* Yes.—

ASAGAI :Well . . . it is true that this is not so much a profile of a Hollywood queen as perhaps a queen of the Nile— But what does it matter? Assimilationism is so popular in your country.

BENEATHA :I am not an assimilationist! (62-63)

Though Asagai says it in a lighter vein but it affects Beneatha deeply. Later Beneatha cuts her hair short. Her act shows that she is an anti-assimilationist who values her culture and African roots and reclaims her identity as a Black.

In *Les Blancs*, Tshembe's brother, Abioseh is an assimilationist who consciously opts for western culture by becoming a Catholic Priest. He preaches "white man's" gospel which is contrary to the message of salvation of his own people:

TSHEMBE: . . . It is your place to wear the robe now. . . .

ABIOSEH: I take the final vows in the spring.

TSHEMBE: And what will your name then, my brother?

ABIOSEH: Father Paul Augustus. I thought to tell you of this in a different way.

TSHEMBE: I see. Such is the marketplace of Empire! You, the son of proud elder of the Kiwi, are now pleased to change your ancient name for that of a Roman Emperor!. . . .

ABIOSEH :Some day a black man will be Archbishop of this Diocese, a black Cardinal. Think of what it will mean!

TSHEMBE. It will mean only the swinging jeweled kettle of incense of another cult—which kept the watch fires of our oppressors for three centuries!

. . . .

TSHEMBE: The sale, dear brother, has been completed and you are wearing the receipts! (62)

Abioseh views are in stark contrast to his brother, Tshembe's who is an anti-assimilationist. Aboiseh is influenced and obsessed with Christian and colonial ways of life which is reflected in his speech and views where he clearly sides with Whites and shows hatred for his own people. And his deception also leads to the murder of Ntali, a leader of resistance. He betrays Ntali by exposing him to Major Rice, a white man who then shoots him dead.

In her play, *Imperceptible Mutabilities*, Parks also explores the issues related to structure of race. Molly consistently practices correct pronunciation in order to be accepted in white society and suppresses her own self and speech to adopt the speech of the affluent class, the white people. Retelling her experience to Charlene, Molly says, "Speak correctly or you'll be dismissed! Yeah. Yeah. Nope. Nope. Job sends me there. Basic skills. Now Job dont want me or more" (26). Molly as a colonized subject undermines her own culture and assumes that black vernacular is not acceptable in American community. Fanon has rightly said:

> The black man speaks with a European language. He becomes proportionately whiter in direct ratio to his mastery of the French language; or indeed, any western language, now a days most particularly English. So, almost immediately, the back man is presented with a problem: how to posit a "black self" in a language and discourse in which blackness itself is at best a figure of absence, or worse a total reversion? (qtd. in Sardar xv)

He adds:

> Overnight the Negro has been given two frames of reference within which he has had to place himself. His

> metaphysics, or, less pretentiously, his customs and the sources on which they were based, were wiped out because they were in conflict with a civilization that he did not know and that imposed itself on him. (Fanon 83)

Later, Charlene talks about Lutzky, the white naturalist and says that he wore white because white is the one that was required for the job. It suggests that Molly and Charlene find it necessary to adapt to a pattern of speech desired by Whites. They purposefully do so for the sake of gaining power and acceptability in American community.

Colonialism and capitalism gripped America for long resulting in economic oppression of African Americans. Classicism became an easy way of posing racial superiority over the other. This ideology advocates that Blacks should be forever available as cheap labour due to which they are always classified as inferior in every aspect especially economically. In *The Wretched of the Earth*, Fanon writes about race and class division:

> . . . . When you examine at close quarters the colonial context, it is evident that what parcels out the world is to begin with the fact of belonging to a given race, a given species. In the colonies the economic sub-structure is also a superstructure . . . you are rich because you are white, you are white because you are rich. (qtd. in Loomba 25)

Race relations are dependent on economic distinctions and economic disparities are determined by race structure. Rex suggests that racism plays a major role in expansion of capitalism:

> When the social order could no longer be buttressed by legal sanctions it had to depend upon the inculcation in the minds of both exploiters and exploited of a belief in the

> superiority of the exploiters and the inferiority of the exploited. Thus it can be argued that the doctrine of equality of economic opportunity and that of racial superiority and inferiority are complements of one another. (qtd. in Loomba 111)

Economic disparity is amongst the recurring themes in the works of Hansberry and Parks. They define the slave trade as the root cause of economic system of Africans and highlight the traumatizing fallouts of racism and slavery. Providing an account of social exploitation of Blacks on the basis of class structure, they have highlighted and very well portrayed the suffering and traumas faced by the Blacks, particularly their economic oppression:

> A pioneering study pointed out that the class relations within which black working-class people exist 'function as race relations. The two are inseparable. Race is the modality in which class is lived. It is also the medium in which class relations are experienced. (Loomba 114)

Parks envisions *Topdog/Underdog* in this light, by depicting it through her protagonist Lincoln who is forced to settle down for less than what a white guy would get for the same job. However, he decides to grab the opportunity for some economic stability in his life:

> LINCOLN:. . . . And as they offered me thuh job, saying of course I would have to wear a little makeup and accept less than what would offer a –another guy –
>
> BOOTH: Go on, say it. "White." Theyd pay you less than theyd pay a white guy. (34)

Lincoln agrees to have his face painted white and wears the makeup. It depicts that black man is forced to put on a mask which is not his authentic self. This is imposed on him through social as well as economic structures in a largely white oppressive society. Parks' drama powerfully foregrounds the intersectionality of race and class. She exemplifies economic oppression in the play by highlighting the lack of space and possessions due to racial barriers. The play focuses on race as the base for contradiction between dreams and reality. As both the brothers struggle against racism and violence for economic stability and power, racial barriers drag them to the lowest position due to financial and occupational constraints, plaguing their lives.

Though the play, *Topdog/Underdog* does not focus on slavery alone, it mirrors the effects of slavery. The adverse conditions under which two brothers, Lincoln and Booth live reflect the devastating effects of slavery, such as racism, discrimination, violence and unequal opportunities. Parks depicts their poor living conditions. The shabby accommodation of a single apartment, without proper water supply, sink and toilet reflects their harsh living conditions. Parks underscores their deprivation through images such as a milk crate converted into a bookshelf the top of which serves as a table to eat their meals and the bottom to store the books. Besides, the brothers live in social isolation. They lead a life deprived of dignity, respect and love. When pain becomes unbearable, they try to assert themselves by raising their voice. In search of dignity and happiness, they strive to acquire social and economic status. In an interview with Susan Lester Cole, Parks maintains, "*Topdog/Underdog* 'is about personal history and family history and about this overriding history that they can't escape" (qtd. in Wetmore Jr and Howard 76). Parks lists Lincoln as 'the topdog' and Booth as the 'the underdog' and relates them to Abraham Lincoln and actor John Wilkes Booth respectively. The term 'dog' is suggestive of their African American status. The void in their lives in respect of social and monetary status is glaring as they live in isolation having been abandoned by their parents at a very early age to live on their own.

Lorraine Hansberry realistically portrays the poor economic condition of Blacks by depicting the minutest details about their actual living conditions in shabby ghettos. Her plays are a powerful comment on the stark reality of the existence of these underprivileged and exploited people. Besides racism and slavery, poverty is an enormous hindrance in the lives of Blacks. *A Raisin in the Sun* gives an authentic description of the Blacks' struggle in an unequal society. Focusing on the lives of the working class families in Chicago's Southside, the play drives home the sordid reality of the ghetto life with the image of a rat. Ruth compares her house to a rat trap. Later, Travis gives his mother a description of the killing of a rat by him and other children, which reflects the poor and dirty environment in which African American children and their families lived. In an interview with Diane Fisher, Hansberry refers to the physical threat one faces in a ghetto, "And the ghetto kills, literally. Statistically, Negro men die the youngest . . . white men, Negro women, and white women follow in that order. I think housing is so important I wrote a play about it" (qtd. in Carter 48). In her play *To Be Young, Gifted and Black*, a letter is quoted which Hansberry wrote to a white woman, Miss Oehler who questioned her for "fuzzy-headed notions of idealism in *A Raisin in the Sun*. Hansberry replied in the letter:

> I absolutely plead guilty to the charge of idealism. But simple idealism. You see, our people don't really have a choice. We must come out of the ghettos of America, because the ghettos are killing us; not only our dreams, as Mama says, but our very bodies. It is not an abstraction to

> us that the average American Negro has a life expectancy of five to ten years less than the average white. You see, Miss Oehler, that is murder, and a Negro writer cannot be expected to share the placid view of the situation that might be the case with a white writer. (131)

An instance in the beginning of the play highlights the degree of economic hardships of the African American family, a theme that runs through the play. In act 1, scene 2, Ruth plans to abort her baby. It is not that she does not want to have a baby but due to their adverse financial condition, she is forced to take such a grave step. She just wants to do the best for the family that she already has. The incident reveals the cruel reality of the curse of utter poverty, which forces a mother, a life giver to destroy her own child:

> MAMA: Son— do you know your wife is expecting another baby? That's what she wanted to talk to you about. This ain't for me to be telling— but you ought to know. I think Ruth is thinking 'bout getting rid of that child.
>
> WALTER: No– no– Ruth wouldn't do that.
>
> MAMA: When the world gets ugly enough – a woman will do anything for her family. The part that's already living.
>
> WALTER: You don't know Ruth, Mama, if you think she would do that.
>
> RUTH: Yes I would too, Walter. I gave her a five-dollar down payment. I gave her a five-dollar down payment.
>
> MAMA: Well–son, I'm waiting to hear you say something . . . I'm waiting to hear how you be your father's son. Be

> the man he was . . . Your wife say she going to destroy your child. And I'm waiting to hear you talk like him and say we a people who give children life, not who destroy them— I'm waiting to see you stand up and look like your daddy and say we done give up one baby to poverty and that we ain't going to give up nary another one . . . I'm waiting. (75)

The ghetto has in fact killed two members of the Younger family— Big Walter and his third child, Claude. Lena tries to convince Walter not to let Ruth have an abortion, and commit another blunder referring to little Claude.

The trauma that black families face due to economic oppression is unambiguously brought to light here. The play refers to the deprivation of Blacks and their access to minimal jobs. Due to societal prejudices, Blacks were not offered good jobs and parity in status. Most of the jobs that they got were menial jobs. This was a major reason behind their miserable socio-economic conditions. The black men would generally be waiters, porters and chauffeurs and the black women were given the jobs of cleaning, cooking, and domestic help. Forced to work as slaves, this was the only means to survive for the Blacks as they were not considered capable of doing anything better. The following words of Lena Younger reflect her anguish in such a scenario:

> My husband always said being any kind of a servant wasn't a fit thing for a man to have to be. He always said a man's hand was made to make things, or to turn the earth with— not to drive nobody's car for em—or—carry they slop jars. And my boy is just like him– he wasn't meant to wait on nobody. (103)

In *Les Blancs,* Tshembe unmasks the myth of race and talks about the political struggles of Blacks while having a conversation with Charlie, a white journalist. When Charlie generalizes that all men are alike and equal and race is unimportant then Tshembe says:

> Race— racism— is a device. No more. No less. It explains nothing. It explains nothing at all . . . It is simply a means. An invention to justify the rule of some men over others . . . And it is pointless to pretend that it doesn't exist – merely because it is a lie! (92)

Tshembe argues that the stratagem of racial discrimination is used to justify the Blacks' exploitation and makes Blacks outsiders in their own land.

The white characters in the play also have different perspectives towards colonialism and racism. Reverend Nielsen is not in favour of educating Africans, so that they remain disempowered and economically unstable. This is borne out by the comments of Willy DeKoven, a doctor in his team:

> DEKOVEN: Mr. Morris, the struggle here has not been to push the African into the Twentieth Century— but at all costs to keep Him away from it! We do not look down on the black because we really think he is lazy, we look down on him because he is wise enough to resent working for us . . .
>
> TSHEMBE: You seem disturb, Mr. Morris –
>
> CHARLIE : . . . Well, it takes a hell of a lot of education to turn a backward people into –How many people in this village can even read?

> TSHEMBE: Read *what?* Drums? Everyone. Books? Six, eight, a dozen at most. . . .
>
> DEKOVEN: Morris, this Mission has been here forty years. It takes perhaps twenty-five to educate a generation. If you look around you will find not one African doctor. Until they govern themselves it will be no different. (114)

Dekoven clearly explains the unkind treatment of Blacks and their everlasting agony. Hansberry unveils the hypocrisy of Whites represented by Neilson who pose to help the downtrodden but actually do nothing productive.

Contestation and Assertion by Blacks

There are various instances of Blacks' defiance under colonial rule and of their struggle and resistance against colonial domination. Rejection of the inferior position and status assigned to Blacks are clearly visible in the instances of insurgence in the texts by black writers:

> The problem Fanon addresses is the constitution of a self-identity where native difference is validated and which empowers the native to rebel. Thus although distancing himself from a rediscovery of tradition which instead of reconceiving and dynamizing the autochthonous culture from within, violently reaffirms customs and beliefs and resumes the worship of ancestors, Fanon argues that such a resurgence assumes an incomparable subjective importance in effecting a break with the colonized condition: 'On emerging from these passionate espousals, the native will have decided . . . to fight all forms of exploitation and of alienation of man.' (Parry 15)

Such an assertive and bold opinion is reflected in Hansberry's and Parks' plays where it is revealed that at one point of time retaliation and assertion are the only tools left with Blacks for survival. Both the writers had a lot in common in respect to their revolutionary spirit and literary aspects. Their characters are seen struggling to find foothold in the revolutionary movement vis-à-vis the traditional characters who represent the conservative ideology. They voice their protest against their exploitation by refusing to be victims and by actively engaging themselves in acts of rebellion. Their plays, therefore, belong to the drama of protest and rebellion where Blacks stand up for their rights. Hence, the black subjects are not portrayed as victims but as the ones who assert and survive the social, cultural and political trauma. Both the playwrights showcase the plight of African Americans brought from Africa and jettisoned in a new land. They highlight the Blacks' alienation from white society and their consistent struggle for survival and identity. Blacks cherish their African culture and advocate respect and love of their own race and culture. In her autobiographical play, *To Be Young, Gifted and Black*, Lorraine Hansberry defines this assertion by depicting what her parents taught her, "we are the products of the proudest and most mistreated of the races of man. . . . And above all there were two things which were never to be betrayed : the family and the race" (48).

Lorraine Hansberry's three plays, *A Raisin in the Sun, The Drinking Gourd* and *Les Blancs* are revolutionary plays for they depict the Blacks' retaliation against colonial powers. These plays aim at the (re)defining the black identity and valuing their presence in America. Hansberry underscores the importance of rebellion for eliminating servitude and gaining liberty.

In *Les Blancs*, after peaceful negotiations for freedom with the white colonialists, Tshembe finally decides to retaliate violently. Hansberry has compared and illustrated the struggle with the story of Hyenas and elephants. Ntali (Peter) makes it clear that dialogues are not enough to attain freedom and narrates the story to Tshembe as to how Modingo, a wise hyena was asked by the other hyenas, the earliest inhabitants of the Jungle, to settle their quarrel with the elephants who demand more space because of their size. Modingo, whose name means "One Who Thinks Carefully Before He Acts" says, "I cannot join you on our side while there is also justice on the other. Let me think on it. And thereupon Modingo thought. And thought . . ."(95). While the hyenas wait for too long, the elephants move in and drive the hyenas out of the Jungle. "That is why the hyena laughs until this day and why it is such terrible laughter: Because it was such a bitter joke that was played upon them while they reasoned" (95). The hyenas symbolize the black man and the elephant the white man. The Whites raped, tortured, lynched, and colonized the black people in their own land. Initially, Tshembe tries to settle down the dispute with his ability to see both sides with love. Tshembe like Modingo, wishes to resolve the conflict through reasoning and hopes to tackle the problems of his people through petitions and discussions in a peaceful manner. But that was not possible. Like the hyena, the black man was there from the beginning. When the white men, like the elephants, gathered together and tried to occupy the place, the black men needed to retaliate and assert for their rights.

Hansberry recalls the history of torture, indignities, and enslavement suffered by the oppressed and justifies violent steps taken by them as an act of affirmation. When Charlie tries to accuse Tshembe of hating all white men, Tshembe laughs and says, “Oh dear God, Why? . . . Why do you all need it so? This absolute lo-o-onging for my hatred! I shall be honest with you, Mr. Morris. I do not “hate” all white men—but I desperately wish that I did” (78).

In *Les Blancs*, a woman warrior appears who symbolizes the spirit of Africa. The Woman encourages Tshembe to be a leader, supporting his people and take a violent action necessary for acquiring freedom. She haunts Tshembe when he refuses to be a part of revolution against western invaders. Tshembe asserts and recoils that he has renounced all spears:

> Tshembe: (*Addressing the WOMAN directly . . .*)NO! I WILL NOT GO! It is not my affair anymore (*She circles in movements symbolic of the life of the people,binding him closer*) I have a wife and son now! (She signifies the slaughter, the enslavement) I know all that . . . I don’t care what happens here . . . I am not responsible! (*She rises: a warrior summoning him urgently, insistently, unrelenting*). . . . I HAVE RENOUNCED ALL SPEARS!!! (*Blackout*). *(81)*

Hansberry presents varied attitudes among the white characters in *Les Blancs*. Dr. DeKoven and Mme. Nielson, an old English woman acknowledge the harm and damage that Reverend Nielson has caused to the Blacks. They support Blacks’ insistence to fight back for their rights. Whereas Mr. Neilson and Dr.Gotterling treat Blacks with contempt, Madam Nielsen compensates for the damage done by her husband by consciously risking her own life and encouraging Tshembe to become a revolutionary and to fight for his land and his people:

> Tshembe: [. . . .] Whether I go or stay, I cannot break open the prison doors for Kumalo. I cannot bring Peter back . . I'm lying Madam, To myself.
>
> And to you. I know what I must do . . .
>
> Madame: Then do it, Tshembe. . . .
>
> Madame: . . . . Our country needs warriors, Tshembe Matoseh. Africa needs warriors.
>
> Like your father. (126)

DeKoven says, "The sun really is starting to rise in the world . . . They are quite prepared to die to be allowed to bring it to Africa. It is we who are not prepared. To allow it or to die" (116). He sympathises with Blacks and admits that he has witnessed the injustice done to the Blacks by the Whites. He is prepared to lay down his life for regaining freedom for them.

Tshembe realizes that he committed a mistake by convincing a resistance leader Ntali (Peter) to talk to colonial government for a peaceful solution which only ended in the martyrdom of Ntali and putting Kumalo, a non-violent leader in jail. Tshembe then decides that the only way to end this problem is through armed resistance. When Charlie tries to convince Tshembe to denounce "terrorism" and support non-violent protest instead, he retorts:

> . . . Mr. Morris your concern for non-violence is little late, don't you think? Where were you when we protested without violence and against violence? We did not hear from you then. Where were you when they were chopping off the right hands of your young men by the hundreds— by the tribe? (91)

Tshembe now firmly believes that talking is not going to help them achieve freedom and equality. He adds:

> Or do you think they have suddenly become impressed because Kumalo is saying the black man wishes freedom? We have been saying that for generations. They only listen now because they are forced to. Take away the violence and who will hear the man of peace? (91)

Similar viewpoint is reflected in *To be Young, Gifted and Black* when Lorraine Hansberry asserts:

> It isn't as if we got up today and said, "What can we do to irritate America?" It's because, since 1619, Negros have tried every method of communication, of transformation of their situation, from petition to the vote—everything –we've tried it all; there isn't anything that hasn't been exhausted. (246)

Hansberry further states:

> I think it's very simple that the whole idea of debating whether or not Negroes should defend themselves is an insult. If anybody comes and does ill in your home or your community—obviously, you try your best to kill him. (249)

Such retaliation is visible in *Les Blancs*, where Blacks' lives are targeted by the invaders, it becomes necessity to resist and revolt. Aboiseh's inappropriate behaviour changes Tshembe from being liberal to being radical. His contemplation to kill his own brother, Aboiseh shows his resistance against anyone who betrayed his people. When he came from America, he was not in support of black rights but when he glimpses the entirety: the destruction of Africa, his mind changes. Thus, the Blacks who once asked for tranquillity and emancipation from the colonialists are now found staging a revolution. The storm of revolution takes into its sweep everyone, not sparing even the innocent people like Madame Nielson and some other white families. By this time, the revolutionary zeal had been so intensified that it had taken the form of never ending White/Black affray. Now Blacks only wish to see the end of colonial rule and the triumph of Blacks over Whites.

In *The Drinking Gourd*, in act 1, a question arises in Sarah's mind and she doubts Hannibal's decision to escape and wonders whether its better now or after freedom:

> Sarah: . . . H'you know its so much better to run off? *(A little desperately, near tears, thinking of the terrors involved)* Even if you make it— h'you know what's up there, what it be like to go wanderin' 'round by yourself in this world?
>
> Hannibal: I don't know. Jes know what it is to be a slave!
>
> Sarah : Where would you go –?
>
> Hannibal: Jes North, that's all I know. . . . There's people up there what helps runaways. (175-76)

Hannibal resents and tells Sarah as to how the slave owners cannot bear the thought of the slaves leaving them. He says:

> That's slave owner talk, Sarah. Whatever you hear Marster say 'bout slavery—you always believe the opposite. There ain't nothin' hurt slave marster so much —as when his property walk away from him. Guess that's the worst blow of all. Way I look at it, ever' slave ought to run off 'fore he die. (176)

The play reflects Hansberry's point of view for equal rights and embodies the revolutionary move. Hannibal tries to convince others around him that it is not justified that one group of people enslave another. He tries to convince his girlfriend, Sarah, to become rebellious. Though nobody supports his revolutionary stride, he does not lose hope. Instead, Hannibal rebels against his mother and master both. In act 2, he screams at his mother Rissa when she tries to convince him to work as a household slave in Hiram's house:

> RISSA: He promised me ever since you was a baby that you wouldn't have to work in the fields.
>
> HANNIBAL: And ever since I could talk I done told you I ain't never goin' be no house servant, no matter what! To no master. I ain't, Mama, I ain't! (200)
>
> He adds:
>
> (Almost screaming) I don't want Marster Everett's bright red jacket and I don't want Marster Sweet's scraps. I don't want nothing' in this whole but to get off this plantation. (201)

Hannibal finally succeeds in putting up a resistance against slavery. In the end, his mother Rissa too, the house slave makes a gesture of defiance against the slave system and black stereotypes by turning her back on her dying master and arming her son for his escape to North, a beacon of freedom. "Wilkerson finds it significant that Hansberry dramatizes the slave's rejection of white authority through the character of Rissa, a woman" (Leeson 74). Rissa possesses the spirit of assertion which eventually leads her to steal Hiram's gun which signifies the breaking of the tyrannical chains which had kept Blacks in bondage for so long. Miller suggests that Rissa is a real human being capable of kindness as well as revenge. The final words of the Soldier/Narrator in the play *The Drinking Gourd* also points towards assertion:

> Slavery is beginning to cost this nation a lot. It has become a drag on the great industrial nation we are determined to become; it lags a full century behind the great American notion of one strong federal union which our eighteenth-century founders knew was the only way we could eventually become one of the powerful nations of the world. And, now, in the nineteenth century, we are determined to hold on to that dream . . . And so— . . . we must fight. There is no alternative. It is possible that slavery might destroy itself— but it is more possible that it would destroy these United States first. That it would cost us our political and economic future . . . It has already cost us, as a nation, too much of our soul. (217)

The recurrent note of assertion by Blacks is evident in Hansberry's *A Raisin in the Sun* as well. The play depicts both black heritage and black resistance to white oppression by different generations. Lena Youngers's decision to buy a house in an all-White neighbourhood unites the family against racism. By refusing the insulting offer of money by Lindner, Walter Lee asserts his pride and his manhood. The resentment is culminated in retaliation and the play ends with the family moving out of the ghetto at last. William B. Collins has rightly observed that there is "something timeless about assertion of pride, about their dignity and their courage as they set out from Chicago's black ghetto for place of their own" (qtd. in Leeson 102).

Thus, the plays of Hansberry are plays of affirmation. Hansberry does not portray the Blacks as pitiable, inarticulate and timid people, but as dignified and courageous people having a voice of their own. Hansberry once said, "The thing I tried to show was the many gradations even in one Negro family, the clash of the old and new, but most of all the unbelievable courage of the Negro People" (qtd. in Carter 22). Lena younger, Walter Lee, Beneatha, Hannibal, Rissa, Tshembe and many other black characters retaliate and assert in the face of oppression. They take a revolutionary stance by raising their voice against exploitation.

Similarly, Suzan-Lori Parks demonstrates that African American history is in itself a sequence of assertions of retrieved experiences. Her work is not confined to portraying Blacks as the oppressed people alone. In her essay "An Equation for Black People Onstage," Parks says, "Can a Black person be onstage and be other than oppressed? For the Black writer, are there Dramas other than race dramas? Does Black life consist of issues other than race issues?" (21).

In *Father Comes Home from the Wars*, in a conversation Smith and Hero contemplate the future of Blacks when they will no longer be slaves, Hero asks Smith the worth of being free:

> Hero: How much you think we're gonna be worth when Freedom comes?
>
> What kind of price we gonna fetch then?
>
> Smith: We won't have a price. Just like they don't. That'll be the beauty of it.
>
> Hero: Where's the beauty in not being worth nothing?
>
> Smith: We won't be able to be moved around, beaten, bought or sold, forced to work and make men rich while we stay poor. . . .
>
> Smith: There is more to Freedom than I can explain, but believe me it's like living in Glory.

Hero: Who will I belong to?

Smith : You will belong to yourself. . . .

Hero: Seems like the worth of a Colored man, once he's made Free, is less than his worth when he's a slave. (96)

Hero is not able to understand the value of becoming a free man which is quite distressing. The play outlines the mental as well as physical agony of a slave. When Smith asks Hero why he has never tried to run away, Hero replies, "Maybe. I'm worth something so me running off would be like stealing" (96). Smith asserts and says that he has full right to steal himself. Fanon rightly observed, "That is why the Negro knows nothing of the cost of freedom; when he has fought for Liberty and Justice . . . these were always white liberty and white justice; that is, values secreted by his masters" (qtd. in Sardar xiii).

Thus, Parks' play not only outlines the theme of assertion for attaining freedom but also focuses on what 'Freedom' actually means. She vividly drafts the implications of freedom in slaves' minds. So insidious is the effect of the institution of slavery that it has seeped into Blacks' mind and soul in such a way that they cannot even glorify freedom. This thought is illustrated by the protagonist of the play who is the representative of all black slaves.

In *The Death of the Last Black Man in the Whole Entire World*, when Voice on the tee V manipulates the facts as it announces the death of the Last Black Man, Prunes and Prisms reacts and says, "oh no no: world is roun" showing their resistance. The play strongly articulates protest against racism and justifies the struggle of Blacks. Death in the play is a metaphor for loss of identity. Writing implies freeing them from oppression for survival in future. The following dialogue between Lots of Grease and

Lots of Pork and Prunes and Prisms depicts the hope for survival and change:

> Yes and Greens Black-eyed Peas Cornbread:You should write that down
>
> . . . This is the death of the Last Man in the whole entire world
>
> Prunes and Prisms: Not Yet. (102)

In *The Death of the Black Man in the Whole Entire World*, Parks focuses on diverse experiences of Blacks. Yes and Greens Black-eyed peas cornbread asserts, "You should write that down . . . And hide it under uh rock" (115).

Parks emphasises on the prerequisite of resistance by the Blacks to be remembered as they know that history of African Americans is erased effectively by white folks. The Black Man urges Black Woman to write down their history because then their struggle, sacrifices and vigilant resistance would be preserved. Hence, writing their experiences affirms their presence, identity and helps them to protect their culture and tradition. He says, "Thuh tongue itself burns" (129). It indicates that if you want to preserve something, you need to write it down otherwise it will vanish or erode with the passage of time. Blacks' endeavour is directed to move from invisibility to visibility and from silence to eloquence. He adds, "My text was writ in water. I would like to drink it down" (116).

Parks believes that it is necessary to rise above the traps of colonialism. Hence, characters' assertion, anger and retaliation time to time bring to the fore the power of Blacks to call action into being. Inhuman treatment meted out by the Whites to Blacks led to strong resentment in the heart of her characters who at last retaliate against the fixed identity assigned to African Americans. In *The Death of the Last Black Man in the Whole Entire World*, Black man commits to come back over and again to his wife in order to narrate his story with assertion. He manages to escape lynching and reconcile with his wife. All this implies that the Black Man will continue to exist through memory. "Although he now rests in peace, Black Man is not dead as long as he lives in Black Woman's—and the audience's—memories" (Larson 25).

In his essay on *Imperceptible Mutabilities*, James Freize acknowledges that "Parks stages dynamic identities that transcend race, and therefore oppression"(117). He further writes:

> To show how Black people carry the relationship to Whites within them, and to think beyond that relationship, Parks dramatizes Black people relating to each other and themselves, trying on Blacknesses which are defining but also mutable. Exhibiting this mutable blackness, Parks's characters first appear conventionally oppressed, but then Parks turns that oppression on its head, transforming them into powerful figures. (qtd. in Wetmore Jr and Howard 117)

Parks showcases the drastic transformation of her characters from conventionally oppressed and suppressed beings to becoming zealous ones. It is reflected very clearly when Black Woman with The Drum sticks says that things are the same in present as they were in the past and would remain the same in future also if Blacks will not assert for their rights by retaliating against the prevalent racial oppression.

Similarly, in *The America Play,* The Foundling Father is very optimistic and hopeful. He says, "Much later when the

Lesser known had made a name for himself he began to record his own movements. He hoped he'd be of interest to posterity. As in the Great Mans footsteps" (162). He records his actions as he wants to make a mark and yearns to be recorded in history and be remembered in future.

In *Imperceptible Mutabilities*, in part3, "Open House," Arthea, asserts to define herself on her own terms, contrary to the misrepresentation of her in official records. She reclaims her power by making an 'historical Amendment,' which leaves Charles powerless. She reverses the role of master and slave:

> Arthea: Don't care what you say done, We're makin us histironical amendment here K? Give us a smile. Uh big smile for thuh book. . . .
>
> Mmmgointuh take my place aside thuh most high
>
> . . . .
>
> Charles: I can't get the children to smile, Ma'am.
>
> Arthea: You smile.
>
> Charles: They're crying, Miss Arthea!. . . .
>
> Arthea: Don't matter none. Don't matter none at all. You say it's uh cry I say its uh smile. These photographs are for my scrapbook.
>
> Scarps uh graphy for my book. (54)

The atrocities faced by Blacks at the hands of Whites have always led to retaliation at one point of time. This is reflected through the character of Arthea who after continuous suffering now refuses to accept any excuses from Charles and rewrites her reality which was destructed by the Whites and was rendered invisible for so long.

In Father Comes Home from the Wars, in part 3, The Union of My Confederate Parts," the chorus of runaway slaves defines the scene of slavery and freedom touchingly. The members of the chorus talk about escaping saying, "You will come with us tonight and wake up in Ohio or California even. Soon to be living in a brand new state where the sun is always shinning" (126).

They flee away taking advantage of the absence of their master and war. In the end Hero says that he has a gift for all the slaves taking out a paper from his pocket— it is Emancipation Proclamation, one of the most idealized and awaited moment of the Civil War which ensures their freedom:

> Ulysses: This paper. I never got to read it to them.
>
> The Proclamation. I copied it down.
>
> It says we're free. (159)

In 1863, Lincoln stated the abolition of slavery explicitly and issued The Emancipation Proclamation. All the abolitionists and free black slaves rejoiced and celebrated the moment.

At the end of the play, Blacks march forward towards freedom, their minds totally liberated now. Death of Colonel, Victory in Civil War, Emancipation Proclamation and their consequent escape from slavery have bought them freedom of their own bodies, souls and mind which were entrapped by the institution of slavery and racism for decades. Their liberty is iconic and symbolizes the advanced life for an entire population of enslaved Blacks.

Thus, both the playwrights endeavour to create an opportunity for Blacks of self-expression against centuries of misrepresentation by interrogating the accepted social norms. Their plays have themes related to assertion of freedom, and creating a future free from the subjugation of the past. They valorize the black heritage/identity harking back to their original state. Their contribution to American drama has been immense in respect of authentic documentation of the actual experiences of Blacks. Vociferously articulating the values, suffering, plight and struggle of African Americans, their prior agenda was not to depict Blacks as oppressed and Whites as oppressors. However, their commitment to bring to the forefront the real social, political and economic situations went a long way in familiarizing the readers with the truth of Black lives.

4
History, Memory, Language and Black Aesthetics

> The perspectives and approaches associated with postcolonial criticism are being used increasingly to address the histories and current predicaments of internally colonized cultures within the nation state in the developed world. (Moor-Gilbert 9)

In the 1960s and early 1970s, African Americans began to show fascination for African culture, language, history and art which facilitated a cultural movement among Blacks in the United States. In the context of socioeconomic, political and cultural systems, historical awareness can open up vistas of connection existing between the living and the dead as well as the present and the past. It can become an important source of power for the present struggle. Walker has rightly said, "I think my whole programme as a writer is to deal with history just so I know where I am" (qtd. in Wisker 38). Any representation of history in a literary text is inseparable from the sphere of politics and society which govern it and the stage is a platform where history can be re-enacted and staged literally.

The influence of Lorraine Hansberry and Suzan-Lori Parks over black theatre and African American literature has been profound. Both the authors' works focus on the importance of African culture and heritage. Their admiration for the black culture is reflected in their works. By presenting history and blackness as complex and powerful signifiers, Hansberry and Parks affirm the power of writing as a cultural code within and as a touchstone of African American experiences. They analyze how African American culture has been reconstructed and redefined within the domain of theatre over a period of time. Lorraine Hansberry and Suzan-Lori Parks were aware that the black writers before them were not equipped to articulate their opinion or didn't have the power to inscribe and publish their history through their works. Both the writers retell their history, with the purpose of highlighting what has been either misinterpreted or left out. They endeavour to represent people, language, politics and cultural traditions that have moulded black people's lives.

Hansberry's experience was twofold. On the one hand, she attended school and fraternized with African Americans, faced discrimination, fought for rights against racism and on the other, as the economic status of her family was good, she did not face any problems that were faced by less fortunate Blacks. To quote Susan Sinnott:

> They seemed like grownups . . . with their ability to fight back, their fierce independence, their street-smarts. They had authority. She, on the other hand, was her family's pet, dressed like a princess to show off her wealth. (qtd. in Secovnie 251)

But Hansberry's experience led her to understand the peculiar intricacies in relation to Blacks and Whites. When Hansberry was working on her plays, *Les Blancs* and *The Sign in Sidney Brustein's Window*, she actively involved herself in the early stages of the Civil Rights Movement. Hansberry puts forth her view vis-à-vis the need for struggle on the part of Blacks:

> Negros must concern themselves with every single means of struggle: legal, illegal, passive, active, violent and non-violent. That they must harass, debate, petition, give money to court struggles, sit-in, lie down, strike, boycott, sing hymns, pray on steps—and shoot from their windows when the racists come cruising through their communities. (qtd. in Secovnie 252)

Hansberry had lived through an era of varied forms of injustice and stood for social changes. She was acutely conscious of the pivotal social and political happenings of the 1950s and 1960s. This period was marked by a rising demand by Blacks for civil rights. Africa in the 1960s was on the verge of revolution. Ghana had emerged in 1957 as the first independent African nation. Jomo Kenyatta, who stood against violence was arrested which led to an exacerbated situation as violence exploded all over the country. Lorraine was a close observer of the trial of Jomo Kenyatta, spokesperson for self-governance in Kenya:

> At street corner meetings in Harlem, as in the pages of Freedom and frequent letters to the press, she questioned whether the trial and in fact the entire British Campaign, was in fact directed at the sporadic and, until Kenyetta's arrest, quite isolated incidents of so called "Mau-Mau" terror. . . . (Nemiroff 30)

Hansberry had always fantasized about the African past and its origin. Like Mau Mau Movement in 1960s, in her play, *Les Blancs*, the tribes were waging silent but deadly warfare against colonists killing them in the dead of night. When nothing could be extracted out of Civil Rights Movement through peaceful means, Blacks were forced to take recourse to rebellion. The play is set in a mythic, African nation, Zatambe ruled by Whites. Hansberry juxtaposes historical facts with dramatic imagination which depicts rebellion and assertion against colonial rule.

After the success of *A Raisin in the Sun,* Hansberry became a more persuasive voice in the American Civil Rights Movement. It gave her a platform to be heard publicly on social issues. She raised her voice against racism and injustice perpetrated on the Blacks. When the play surfaced in 1959, Civil Rights Movement was in its earlier stages. The play reflects the struggle of Blacks in those days. Hansberry spoke at civil rights rallies, gave interviews and speeches. She wrote more than sixty articles in magazines and newspapers and the text of *The Movement: Documentary of a Struggle for Equality*, a photographic essay on the Civil Rights Movement. Hansberry offers an insight of African history in her plays. In her play, *A Raisin in the Sun* through Asagai's speeches about the necessity of emancipating African continent from the clutches of British and French, Hansberry intends to inform the audience about the forgotten African history. Asagai plans to return after his college to contribute to vital social as well as political changes in his native place Nigeria, which was under British colonial rule till that time. Asagai underscores the need to liberate Africa. Beneatha also discusses the same issue with her ignorant mother:

> Mama: Why should I know anything about Africa?
>
> Beneatha: Why do you give money at church for missionary work?
>
> Mama: Well, that's to help save people.
>
> Beneatha: You mean save them from heathenism—
>
> Mama (Innocently): Yes

Beneatha: I'm afraid they need more salvation from British and the French. (57)

Hansberry has dealt with actual and existing issues like segregation, slavery and Civil War in her plays while depicting the historical past of Blacks. The plays *A Raisin in the Sun* and *The Drinking Gourd* dramatize the slave institution and analyse the history of American slavery from its beginning. Hansberry depicts the multi-generational aspect of Blacks' history pertaining to dreams, struggle, frustration and hopes.

A Raisin in the Sun presaged the rampant transformation in black and feminist movements and appears as a literary impetus of the Black Arts Movement (BAM) of the 1960s. She emphasizes the need for Blacks to liberate themselves from the clutches of white dominance. In her iconic plays, *A Raisin in the Sun* and *Les Blancs*, Hansberry has depicted Blacks' dream for equality and separate identity. She highlights the pride and value of the African heritage, the main idea promoted by Black Arts Movement. Asagai always discusses black roots and inspires Beneatha to embrace her culture and follow her dreams. He teaches her about African culture to make her understand her true identity. Beneatha appreciates Asagai's views and likes his company as he always tries to rediscover their African roots. Contrary to Asagai and Beneatha's views, George is an assimilationist who does not value and respect the African heritage. Beneatha asserts that she hates assimilationist Negroes and says, " . . . See there . . . you are standing there in your splendid ignorance talking about people who were the first to smelt iron on the face of the earth!" (81).

The play *A Raisin in the Sun* foreshadows the interracial as well as intraracial deliberations around the politics of racial oppression and race representation. Amiri Baraka observes, "as a document reflecting the essence of [civil rights] struggles, the play is unexcelled . . . it remains the quintessential civil rights drama" (qtd. in Davis and Skinner348). Hansberry depicts the representation of blackness in the play and illustrates how history shapes these representations. The quest for political and social equality, assertion and the early Civil Rights Movement are the major themes in the play. John McClain contends in Journal American:

> A small hunk of history was made . . . last night. A play by a Negro about Negroes with an almost all Negro cast opened on Broadway and was a stupendous unsegregated hit. It proved to me at least, that when these people create and participate in something for themselves, they can make the rest of us look silly. (qtd. in Page 360)

Tracing back vital episodes of African American history, — Hansberry tries to bring to the fore the dynamics of racism and colonialism. She juxtaposes the past and present in her plays, *A Raisin in the Sun, The Drinking Gourd and Les Blancs.* They can be categorized as revolutionary plays as they re-evaluate the existence of Blacks in America. In *Les Blancs*, Hansberry powerfully articulates the struggles of the black people. Tshembe, who has lived in Europe with his wife returns to Africa and tries to reclaim his identity by choosing to stay in Africa and serve his people. He also takes an anti-assimilation stance just like Beneatha and Asagai in *A Raisin in the Sun.* Amiri Baraka explains:

> We thought Hansberry's play was part of the 'passive resistance' phase of the movement" and realized later, "We missed the essence of the work—that Hansberry had created a family on the cutting edge of the same class and ideological struggles as existed in the movement itself and

> among the people." He now sees the play as "the accurate telling and stunning vision of the real struggle. (qtd. in Bloom 13)

Similarly, Suzan-Lori Parks emerges as one of the most innovative dramatists of her times in so far as her technique is concerned. Her plays restructure the conventional construction of history of black people. Parks started her career at the close of the twentieth century and the beginning of the twenty first century. She has a deep connection with both the eras. Parks' works can be viewed as both a product of the black history and the expression of post-modernism's captivation with displacement and shifting identities. Her oeuvre mainly deals with the black and female identity. Her events and characters reflect both black cultural history and contemporary postmodernism. Parks deals with the issues such as memory, death and desires in context of race and gender identity. Portraying her characters as icons of Blacks' conventional roles, she recalls their painful memories. As Carole Boyce Davies rightly says:

> Because we were/are products of separations and dislocations and dis-memberings, people of African descent in the Americas historically have sought reconnection. From the "flying back" stories which originated in slavery to the "Back to Africa" movements of Garvey and those before him. . . . need to re-connect and re-member, as Morrison would term it, has been a central impulse in the structuring of Black thought. (12)

Parks writes, "History is time that won't quit" (15). She suggests the necessity to write the history for African Americans because during slavery, Blacks were not even allowed to be literate and thus were not able to pen their views and experiences. She chronicles the composite phenomena of history, memory and culture. By retelling the stories, Parks reclaims the greatness of the past and reconstructs the lost or hidden black thought. She emphasizes on reshaping and bringing back the African American history to life by rewriting the dismantled elements of history by the Whites. Her plays ingrain the icons of remembering, re-membering and dis-membering the black history by (re)reading and (re)writing of history from an altogether new perspective, adding new significations as well as meaning to it. To quote Kimberly d. Dixon:

> Finally, I consider Parks' work to be, to borrow Sydné Mahone's words, "compelling, thought-provoking and stylistically fresh." Her work demands the spectator's and reader's full attention with an intricacy of language and action that invites second and third interpretations. (221)

These second or third interpretations certainly invite the spectators and the readers to re-evaluate history from Parks' perspective. Parks gained a significant position during the 1990s in American literature for being a distinct voice as she highlights the relationship between history and theatre and thus insightfully pinpoints that Blacks have been misrepresented as their history is not written by themselves but by the Whites, which is a mythical and fabricated version.

African American literature has been shaped by the history of African Americans which is a direct consequence of the effects of colour based discrimination within America. In her essay "Possession," Parks complains about how African American history has been dismembered and erased. She says, "The history of literature is in question. And the history of History is in question too. A play is a blueprint of an event: a way of creating and rewriting history through the medium of literature" (Parks 4). She attempts in her plays to dig, recover and retell the forgotten history of black workers and their plight. She picks up a few historical events and reframes them by bringing to the forefront the absent elements through her narratives.

In *The Death of the Last Black Man in the Whole Entire World*, Parks recreates the image of the Ohio River through Old Man River Jordan who had witnessed the agonies of runaway slaves' in crossing the river to escape slavery. He says, "Uhcrossthuh river in back tuh that . . . . He backs his way through tall grass. Grass thickly comin from all angles at im. He runs along thuh path worn out by uh 9 million paddlin bare footed feet" (114). Parks relates Black Man with Watermelon's plight to runaway slaves' efforts to attain liberty, which further illustrates their agonies. In the play, he becomes the medium for slaves to show them the way to escape.

In *The Death of the Last Man in the Whole Entire World*, the major focus is on writing down things so that Blacks can be remembered and their existence can be assured, which points towards the significance of documentation of events which is necessary as evidence for an authentic history to be written. Parks explicitly attacks Whites who do not acknowledge Blacks' presence in the past: "if you don't write it down then they will come along and tell the future that we didn't exist" (104). Parks plays' strongly reflect the importance of writing as to keep African American heritage alive, so that it can be preserved for the future generations who would otherwise have known nothing about them. History is (re)stored as they say:

> . . . hide it under a rock or carve it out of rock. You will write down thuh past and you will write down thuh present

> and in what in thuh future. You will write it down . . . when they come along they'll know how they exist. . . . the rock does yes exist. (130-31)

Parks recollects the past experiences of Blacks and reshapes it by surpassing the previous history and recreating a new history. She brings to the forefront various instances of historical and contemporary black invisibility. Through following conversation, Parks alludes to the distortion and exclusion of a black existence:

> YES AND GREENS BLACK-EYED PEAS CORNBREAD: Whatcha seen hambone girl?
>
> BLACK WOMANWITH FRIED DRUMSTICK: Didntsee you. I saw thuhworl.
>
> QUEEN-THEN-PHARAOH HATSHEPSUT: I was there.
>
> Lots of grease and lots of pork: Didnt see you.
>
> BLACK WOMAN WITH FRIED DRUMSTICK : I was there.
>
> BLACK MAN WITH WATERMELON: Didnt see you. The black man moves his hands.
>
> QUEEN-THEN-PHARAOH HATSHEPSUT : We are too young to see. Let them see it for you. We are too young to rule. Let them rule it for you. (103-04)

Parks is of the view that history written by the Whites does not record everything. She challenges and endeavours to transform the existing metanarratives by viewing history from various angles and from different lenses. She represents her characters from different places, ages and eras. Heidi J. Holder says: "The connections and parallels between the events of the past and the conditions of the present are often made explicit rather than implicit" (qtd in Wetmore Jr and Howard 18). Parks' focus is not confined to depicting the phase of Blacks' exploitation only in one period but all periods of time. By doing so, she endeavours to liberate the entire black community from an unjust treatment meted out to them in history. The purpose of her plays is to fill up the blank spots, unearth the untold stories of the past that are hidden.

Parks introduces in some of her plays the theme of the Great (W)hole of history. In *The America Play*, there is a theme park called the Great Hole of History. The play holds on to an African American content and theme within the sedate notion of performing:

> It is a history that is in reality an absence, because the national mythology or history has been created by Whites. . . . The theme of the play is that Europeans stole not only Africa's people, wealth, and minds, but also its history. (Huskey 461)

Parks presents the play as a replica of the great hole of history and includes the recorded as well as unrecorded history. She tries to fill some parts of the Great Hole of History and make some space for Blacks who have been rendered voiceless and invisible otherwise. She allows her audience to imagine the past in the present by placing a black gravedigger as an impersonator of Lincoln and attempts to recreate the history. In the very beginning of play, Foundling Father finds himself in a great hole. Parks defines the place, "A great hole. In the middle of nowhere. The hole is an exact replica of The Great Hole of History" (158). The Foundling Father repeatedly re-enacts Lincoln's death and digs a replica of the "great hole of history," which drags him into the past from the present. "He digged the hole and the whole held him" (159). He describes his detachment from the self and from history.

> Not a hole he had digged but one he'd visited. . . . A Big Hole. A theme park.The size of the hole itself was enough to impress any Digger but it was the historicity of the place the order and beauty of the pageants which marched by them the Greats on parade in front of them. . . . The Hole and the historicity and the part he played in it all gave a shape to the life and posterity of the Lesser Known that he could never shake. (162)

Likewise, in act 2, Brazil, Foundling father's son, is compelled by Lucy, Foundling father's wife, to dig, which depicts that she wants to know the truth about the ancestors and the past. Digging signifies exploration of past for legacy and recognition. Brazil continues to dig in the very hole:

> Lucy: Dig on, Brazil Can't stop digging till you dig up somethin.
>
> Your Daddy was uh Digger. . . .
>
> Lucy:. . . . His lonely death and lack of proper burial is our embarrassment. Go on: dig. Now me I need to know thuh real thing from thuh echo. Thuh truth from thuh hearsay. (174-75)

Lucy further illustrates the misinterpretation of history which prevents her from making any claims, even when her son insists:

> Brazil: You hear him then? His whispers?
>
> Lucy: Not exactly.

> Brazil: He wuduhnt here then.
>
> Lucy: He was here.
>
> Brazil: Ffyoudont hear his whispers he wuduhnt here.
>
> Lucy: Whispers dont always come up right away. Takes time sometimes. Whispers could travel different out West than they do back East. . . . We also could be experiencing some sort of interference. . . . So much to live for. (178)

Through the continual digging by the Foundling Father and later by his son, Parks unfolds the continuous hard work of African American slaves and at the same time depicts the power of the history and cultural memory.

In *The Death of the Last Man in the Whole Entire World*, through her characters, Parks talks about the holes in history and seeks to rewrite history from a new perspective. Parks brings to the fore past, present and future together by depicting deaths, oppression and agonies that Blacks have endured since ages till the present time and will be facing in future as well if they choose to remain silent. The play introduces the plight of the Black man, forerunner of the Civil Rights Movement who is captured, enslaved, auctioned, tortured and lynched by the Whites. The repeated deaths of the Black Man represent the brutal violence imposed on Blacks throughout history.

Parks represents the Black Man's history and experience in particular and the entire black community in general. The Black Man in *The Death of the Last Black Man in the Whole Entire World* represents the period of slave plantations as well as the contemporary times. Parks draws a parallel between the period of slavery and the present-day condition of the slaves in America. One of the most pertinent aspects of black history depicted in the play is the lynching of Blacks. The Black man dies different deaths, he is hanged on a tree, he is cut down, he jumps into a river and falls from twenty-three floors. Many more cruelties are perpetrated on him. The play showcases Blacks' struggle for equality, justice, literacy, equal rights and above all survival. The death of the Black Man is symbolic of the world view of the whole community. Likewise, the survival and existence of the Black man is interpreted as essential for the whole community.

In her play *Venus*, Parks resurrects the true story of Saartjie Baartman. Parks reframes it with the main focus to connect the past to the present adding new mini narratives in order to fill in the hidden and the lost parts with a minimum fictionalization. Besides, Parks has made an extensive use of various historical and medical excerpts which are included in footnotes, Historical Extract, Category: Medical. Autopsy report: "Her brain, immediately after removal, deprived of the greater part of its membranes, weighed 38 ounces" (37). Parks has given the references of advertisements and paragraphs of newspapers from Daniel Lysons Collectanea pertaining to multiple Subjects. "Footnote#4/Historical Extract: Category: Newspaper Advertisement. . . ." (53). Though Parks' use of footnotes makes it complex, it leads to authenticity of facts given in the text.

Parks chronicles the life of Venus and allows her to speak, "After 500 years they allowed her to ask a question. She wanted to know what her crime had been" (67). Parks deliberately incorporates history in her play, though she invests Venus with a power to resist as a black woman. She gives her a voice, which was absent in the past. Venus' plight has been depicted from her own perspective which is the perspective of the black people. By providing an authentic view of history, Parks brings to life the deliberate suppression of facts about the Blacks' past. Viewed from this perspective, Parks' recreating history is a site of reminiscence and resistance to assert the Blacks' dignity and identity. Interrogating the history written by the Whites, Parks throws light on those events and facts which had been rendered invisible by the predominant culture.

Parks emphasizes the need to view Blacks as normal human beings. She asserts that Blacks can be defined as well as presented onstage in multiple ways: "We have for so long been an 'oppressed people, but are Black people only blue?'" (19). Parks makes it clear that the black people are not to be identified only by their race and culture but by virtue of their individual personalities just like the Whites. She dismantles the stereotypes of perception of traditional black aesthetic.

Parks portrays strong and bold characters who articulate and recreate history and rejoice in their story. In her essay "Elements of Style," Parks describes her characters and states: "they are not characters. To call them so could be an injustice. They are figures, figments, ghosts, roles, lovers maybe, speakers maybe, shadows, slips, players maybe, maybe someone else's pulse" (12). In her play, *Imperceptible Mutabilities in the Third Kingdom*, through Veronica, Parks implicitly expresses the idea that Whites and Blacks are the same beneath the skin. Veronica talks about a black dog that was brought to her hospital, where she works:

> Someone brought a stray dog in one day and I entered "black dog" in the black Book. . . . Wiped her out! I stayed late that night so that I could cut her open because I had to see the heart of such a disagreeable domestic thing. But no. Nothing different. Everything in its place. Do you know what that means? (36-37)

Similar viewpoint is expressed in *Venus* also, where a black woman faces racial inequality in social domains. Whites treat Blacks as inferior and objectify them, which is reflected through the footnotes in the play itself:

> THE VENUS HOTTENTOT
>
> THE ONLY LIVING CREATURE OF HER KIND IN THE WORLD
>
> STEPSISTER-MONKEY TO THE GREAT
>
> LOVE. (45)

It is further depicted as to how even after the abolition of slavery, the Blacks were humiliated and exploited by the Europeans:

> Early in the present century a poor wretched women was exhibited in England. . . . With an intensely ugly figure, distorted beyond all European notions of beauty . . . she belonged to possess precisely the kind of shape which is most admired among her countrymen, the Hottentots. The year was 1810, three years after the Bill for the Abolition of the Slave-Trade had been passed in Parliament and among protests and denials, horror and fascination, the Venus show went on. (46)

Historically slaves were renamed by their masters with Americanised names which most of the Blacks were not willing to accept in order to retain their own identity. For example, Malcon X revoked the surname given by Whites. He said, "For me, my 'X replaced the white slavemaster name of 'Little' which some blue eyed devil named Little had imposed upon my paternal forebears" (qtd. in Goto 116). Likewise, Parks also illustrates it in some of her plays. In *Imperceptible Mutabilities in the Third Kingdom*, part 1:"Snails," Chona instructs Mona to sign Dr. Lutzky's extermination invoice:

> Lutzky : Here is my invoice. Sign here.
>
> Chona: X, Mona. Help Yourself.
>
> Mona: Splat. . . .
>
> Lutzky: What did you claim your name was dear?
>
> Mona: Splat. (35)

Here 'X' signifies the rejection of her slave name. The 'Americanised' names were also given to the slaves so that the Whites could claim them as their properties. Arthea was also named as Arthea Saxon. To quote Andrea J. Goto, "Saxon refers to the Germanic portion of the term 'Anglo-Saxon' which denotes the white colonizers of America" (116).

John Edgar Wideman prefaces his novel *Sent For You Yesterday* with this testament:

> Past lives in us, through us. Each of us harbours the spirits of people who walked the earth before we did, and those spirits depend on us for continuing existence, just as we depend on their presence to live our lives to the fullest. This insistence on the inter-dependence of past and present is, moreover, a political act, for it advocated a revisioning of the past as it is filtered through the present. (qtd. in Rushdy 140)

Parks reconstructs the past events and experiences by analysing them with more critical eyes and envisions Blacks from an entirely new perspective. She believes that Blacks have their own identity, different and separate from the Whites, so their existence should not be dependent on the comparison with the Whites. She attempts to alter the tradition of looking at Blacks only in relation to Whites and she emphasizes the need to change the long lived culture of representing Blacks always as sufferers and 'the other'. Parks' revisionary aesthetic is wholly innovative rather than just an imitation. She reveals the forgotten aspect of the text and uncovers the new dimensions which are open to interpretations.

In an interview with Kevin J. Wetmore, Suzan-Lori Parks clears her position about the reconstruction of the history and the old texts:

> KJW: Bonnie Metzgar calls *In the Blood* a 'now play'. But you're known for history plays. So 'now' means 'history'?
>
> SLP: Well, I'm known for history plays, but actually, the plays were never 'history plays'. Like Faulkner says 'History is *IS*'. So my plays often feature historical figures. But they're all 'now' plays. . . . to me, the plays have never been history plays. They're all about the intersection of the historical and the now. Even *In the Blood* is about that intersection because it is not based on *The Scarlet Letter* but *The Scarlet Letter* is one of its parents, let's say. (qtd. in Wetmore 133)

In *Topdog/Underdog*, Parks repeats history. The character Lincoln rehearses the death of the American President Abraham Lincoln at home and dies repeatedly at work as it is the demand of his job. Here Parks focuses on the dynamic structuring that affects the lives of black people due to economic degradation and prolonged racism. Parks rewrites the assassination of Abraham

Lincoln in *The America Play* as well where Lincoln is represented the same as the President except in terms of his race. He quits his previous job where he was a gravedigger and starts working as an actor recreating the assassination of Lincoln. Thus, the events of the past are recreated again and again in the present.

In *Imperceptible Mutabilities* in part 3, subtitled as "Open House," Parks reconstructs the traumatic memory of the agonizing past of the black slaves that they underwent during and even after slavery. Parks throws light on the objectification of a black woman slave who is stamped as expired as she grew old. The date of expiry of Arthea is depicted as 19th June,1865 which refers to the abolition of slavery. Miss Faith reads Footnotes, "Juneteenth 1865, was when, a good many months after the Emancipation Proclamation, the slaves in Texas heard they were free. You expire. Along with your lease . . . with no option to renew" (47). She further alludes to the amendment XIII that abolished slavery in US through Miss Faith, who keeps on referring to it:

> Miss Faith: Amendment! Amendment XIII. You have been extracted from the record, Mrs. Saxon. You are free. You are clear. You may go.
>
> Arthea: Free and clear to go. Go. (52)

Whites erased the history of Blacks and placed them in a miserable position in American history. Parks tries to restore history through memory. In "Open House," Arthea reclaims her past and her identity through memory. Miss Faith says, "You expire –Yes Maam!. . . . Youre expiring. It's only natural. That's a fact. Amendment 1807" (47). Her statement depicts Whites' attempt to erase black identity and obliterate Blacks' resistance from the pages of history.

Simone Weil has rightly said, "To be rooted is perhaps the most important and least recognized need of the human soul" (qtd. in Rodriguez and Fortier 7). Writing enables us to resist the existing dominant discourses as it contributes to awareness and a worthwhile present and future. In one of the most famous uses of chiasmus in American literature, Douglass prepares the conversion scene: "You have seen how a man was made a slave; you shall see how a slave was made a man" (qtd. in Ross 154).

Collective memories that are culturally constructed over a period of time play an integral role in the shaping of African American identities. Morrison writes, "It is an instrument that can be traced back to African heritage: "it's true what Africans say: "The Ancestors live as long as there are those who remember" (qtd. in Rushdy 149).

Cultural Memory: Saga of struggle and survival

Mary Frances Berry and John Blassingame writes, "Memory itself is for African-Americans 'an instrument of survival" (qtd. in Morrison 149). History and cultural memory are closely intertwined as history is moderately an account of eyewitness and partly uncovers the memories of those who had experienced the events. Cultural memory tends to preserve knowledge about history and culture for future generations to understand and reframe their own cultural identity. It particularly informs about the oppression, atrocities and struggle for survival. It provides immense support for the survival of community which is marginalised historically, politically and socially from the past years by unfolding the saga of diminished groups who strived hard to uphold the social construct to exist in the world and depict their resistance against dominant forces:

> [. . .] never fight against memory. Even if it is painful, it will help you: it will give you something, it will enrich you. Ultimately, what would culture be without memory? What would philosophy be without memory? What would love be . . . ? One cannot live without it. One cannot exist without remembrance. (Rodriguez and Fortier 9)

From one generation to the other, from the past to the present and the future, cultural memory transmits the significance of tradition, culture, dignity and communal experience, which is very poignantly illustrated by Hansberry in her plays. *A Raisin in the Sun* depicts how Younger family faced many hurdles due to racism. Walter had seen his parents being treated with indignity. It was the bitter memories of these experiences that led to his retaliation against Whites. Walter tells Linder, "We have decided to move into our house because my father—my father—he earned it for us brick by brick. . . . We don't want your money" (148). Walter's childhood experience and remembrance moulded his character. Lena tells Walter to uphold the respectful memory of their ancestors and set up an example for his son, Travis and future generations. Walter says to Linder, ". . . . we come from people who had a lot of pride. I mean—we are very proud people" (148).

Cultural memory emphasizes that the present is irreversibly constructed by the recollections of the past events and history. It works as a barricade of resistance to and thus leads to the survival of the community in the present as well as the future. Narrative acts as the tool from which cultural memory paves its way to connect with people. It acquaints the community with their past history and existence. Narratives integrate the recollected past, give it meaning and become the voice and the strength of the people.

The cultural memory is manifested in the usual forms of African American music and speech. It carries the fragments of rich African-ness expressed in the most appropriate way in the present time:

> The Cultural memory of Africa gains its unique power . . .by being located in the interstices of narrative language, the spaces where past becomes present and present becomes future, offering in these spaces exciting possibilities for cultural identity in the twentieth and twenty first centuries. (Kamali 12)

Cultural memories are passed from generation to generation through the medium of oral tradition, folklore, written accounts, rituals, myths, stories, symbols, etc. carrying forward the individual as well as communal experiences of people which are never stagnant and lends meaning to the present. Well cultivated memories may help people not only to deal with difficult situations but also to get over them.

One of the most important aspects of cultural memory is folklore. Folklore plays an empowering role in African American Literature. As Blacks were not allowed to be educated, they could hardly read or write, the only medium to convey social rituals, traditions, culture, etc. was by word of mouth. African American authors continued the legacy and have assimilated the folklore into their texts to preserve traditional values, voice their opinion against racial inequality, and express themselves and pass on messages. Folklore, therefore, becomes a mark of assertion. It is vital in sustaining the history, beliefs, tales and values of a community:

> Folklorist Dan Ben-Amos has referred to folklore simply as, "artistic communication in small groups," while Robert

> Baron and Nicholas Spitzer have argued that "while folklore is private and intimately shared by groups in formal settings, it is also the most public of the activities when used by groups to symbolize their identity to themselves and others. (qtd. in Turner 200)

Folklore in African American texts serves the purpose in a dual manner: aesthetic as well as socio-cultural plans. "Folklore includes legends, superstitions, songs, tales, proverbs, riddles, spells . . . customary activities at births, marriages and deaths; and traditional dances. . . . " (Abrams100). Hansberry and Parks employ the folklore abundantly in their literary works to explore the issues pertaining to racial identity, equality and freedom.

Hansberry incorporates black folklore as a way to recover an African American culture and depicts its significance. In her play *Les Blancs,* Hansberry incorporates various forms of folklore, including mysticism, vision of Africa, primitivism, myths, etc. She attempts to redefine Africa to show the glorious past and cultural memories of African Americans. Hansberry employs African myths in the play related to the rites of death:

> TSHEMBE:. . . . Tell me about my father in his last hours. Of what things did he speak?
>
> ERIC: Only of his ancestor, what else?
>
> TSHEMBE: Why do you say it like that, Eric?
>
> ERIC:. . . . He was just an old savage who went to his death rubbing lizard powder on his breast and chanting out his Kula or some damn thing! (57)

Myths and folklore serve as vehicles of guidance as Hansberry tries to redefine or correct the past:

> Cheney notes Hansberry's finesse in underpinning the realistic drama of *Les Blancs* with Old African myths that signify profound rites of passage through which both Africans and their emerging countries must proceed. Not only do death and initiation rites add depth and deep human and cultural significance to Tshembe's experience, but the mystical and beautiful Woman who appears in the play reminds him, and the audience, of his primal heritage. (qtd. in Leeson 65)

In *A Raisin in the Sun*, Hansberry portrays a revolutionary model for Blacks, Asagai, a Nigerian character who familiarizes the audience to variant aspects of African heritage as well as tradition. He emphasizes on the significance of Black Culture and enlightens Beneatha about the rich African heritage, beliefs and values. He gifts her a Nigerian robe:

> Asagai:. . . . So—you like the robes? . . . they are from my sister's personal wardrobe.
>
> Beneatha: You—You sent all the way home—for me? . . . .
>
> (*She picks up the Nigerian dress and holds it up to her in front of the mirror. . . . Then she starts to wriggle in front of the mirror as she thinks a Nigerian woman might*). (63-66)

Lorraine Hansberry was proud of her African American identity which was inseparable from her and is reflected very profoundly in her works.

Memory is a key term in Parks' plays as well. She refers to remembering/ disremembering with the idea that whatever has happened in the past, must occur repeatedly which she showcases through the technique of rep. & rev. She depicts the disconnected aspect of history in her essay "Possession." And writes:

> memory
>
> un-remembered
>
> dis-membered
>
> re-member
>
> "his bones cannot
>
> be found"
>
> Putting the body
>
> back together. (Parks 5)

Parks adds, "Through each line of text I'm rewriting the TimeLine –creating history where it is and always was but has not yet been divined" (5). The characters in *The Death of the Last Black Man in the Whole Entire World* tell stories to each other from time to time which reflect their cultural ties. Folkloric nature of the characters unites them to take a firm stand against the atrocities perpetrated upon them. Their stories ensure their struggle and endurance.

Writing (re)stores the history of African Americans. The act of remembering is emphasised by Parks through her black characters: how they were tortured and lynched. Parks discusses the African American cultural memory through an extended focus upon the nature of slave tradition. She specifically refers to African born slaves struggling for their existence and to be alive. In *The Death of Last Black Man in the Whole Entire World,* the figure says, "Hold it" and repeats it several times. Parks emphasises that what has been saved or stored should be turned into a memory.

She intends to recover what has been erased from African American history by using archaeological analogy of 'digging for bones.' She endeavours to counteract the effects of predominant historical discourses which have tended to wipe out the African American history. Since the Blacks are not given equal status, Parks tries to recreate the historical narratives from which earlier Blacks were displaced by rewriting history. She digs deep down to excavate the blurred black history.

Parks' dramaturgy of restoring history includes her technique of "rep. & rev." In her essay "Elements of Style,"Parks observes, "Rep & Rev is a concept integral to the Jazz aesthetics in which the composer or performer will write or play a musical phrase once and again and again; etc –with each revisit the phrase is slightly revised" (8-9). Parks seeks the idea of not only rewriting the history but she enacts, re-enacts the events with a revision in her plays. She repeats the scenes and dialogue in her plays many times with some revision and variation. As noted by Jr. & Krasner, "In *Black Looks: Race and Representation*, hooks describes "critical remembering" as a way to interrogate the past" (Kranser 229).

Parks explains in an interview in the *Austinist*:

> I bought a Kids book about Abraham Lincoln, a picture book. There he was, looking skinny and worried. But the plays have less to do with Lincoln and more to do with the memory of Lincoln. . . It's the past in the present moment. It's not just looking back. It's the past as it explodes into the present. When we remember, we're literally putting the members back together, putting our bodies back together. (qtd. in Kolin 13)

Parks uses "Rep & Rev" technique in her play, *Father Comes Home from the Wars* to signify the importance of cultural stories highlighting the oral storytelling tradition. The Chorus of Runaway Slaves in part 3:

> FIRST: You haven't heard the old stories
>
> But I have.
>
> SECOND: You don't know the old stories
>
> But I do.
>
> THIRD: Old stories, they guide us
>
> Each its own North Star
>
> You don't know them
>
> And how could you?
>
> SECOND: They happened so far back
>
> FIRST: Years ago
>
> THIRD: Years and years ago
>
> SECOND: Years and years and years ago
>
> THIRD: What could they have to do with you? (151)

It throws light on the Americans' hypocrisy in the era of slavery and pinpoints the revolutionary struggle for liberty. Memory helps Blacks to interpret the historical past and shape the future. As Douglass contended, "We have to do with the past only as we can make it useful to the present and to the future" (qtd. in Gorden 153).

In *Imperceptible Mutabilities*, Parks showcases the reality and image of Africa. In "Snails," Verona tells her first knowledge and memory of Africa:

> I saw my first pictures of Africa on TV: Mutual of Omahas Wild Kingdom . . . . It was wonderful world: Marlin Perkins and Jim and their African guides. I was a junior guide and had a life size poster of Dr. Perkins sitting on a white Land Rover surrounded by wild things. . . . Black folks with no clothes. Marlin loved and respected all the wild things. (36)

She remembers Africans as romanticized objects of the white adventurous glance. The indigenous people are shown as barbarian and savage ones, without any clothes. Verona is surrounded with the question related to Blacks' inferiority and relates it to the present reality. She is horrified by such kind of disparaging and restricted portrayal of Blacks.

In "Open House," Arthea acknowledges that there is a profound reflection and role of the past in the present, especially in formation of the identity. The memories of the past and the individual's identity are interlinked at a collective level. John Locke aptly observes:

> There is no such thing as an essential identity, but that identities have to be constructed and reconstructed by acts of memory, by remembering who one was and by setting this past Self in relation to the present Self. (qtd. in Erll 6)

The play focuses on the history of inhumanity. Memory enlivens the present and can lay down some rules for the future. Charles Saxon who is White also puts emphasis on the importance of memory. He says, "Memory is a very important thing, don't you know. It keeps us in line. We would be running about here with no identities" (48). There is an indication in the play that Arthea is married to Charles Saxon, her master. This thought takes us back to the history of the period of slavery, when a black woman slave married to a white master was not treated as a wife but as a property to be raped and sexually exploited by her master. Their marriage was not considered legal ever.

Arthea while leaving, asks children to smile and says, "Smile or no smile, mm gonna remember you. Mm gonna remember you grinning" (54). Thus, Arthea remembers and records her own history her own way:

> Black abolitionists such as Garnet, Delany, and Douglass insert an alienated, historical, material, collective, black, public voice into America's public dialogue so as to mediate America's past, challenge the un-American story of exclusion, and tell a different story. (Gorden 154)

Lorraine Hansberry and Suzan-Lori Parks, like Garnet and Douglas reconstruct Blacks' dignified identity which was distinct from the one constructed by the White America. Douglass' speech, "What to the Slave Is the Fourth of July?" was addressed to a predominantly white audience. As Gordon observes:

> With his focus on the promise of America, Douglass provided a black perspective that served as a counterpoint to the largely separatist agendas of Garnet and Delany. . . . Douglass projected a more hopeful, integrated future for America, a future in which blacks did not yield their rights to America or claim allegiance to Africa in contrast to America. Instead, Douglass's black subject contended for both its "Americanness" and its "Africanness" in one

> paradoxical, contorted, but distinctly human being. (157-58)

Hansberry and Parks affirm varied experiences of the Blacks' past to re-create their culture and history. Black memory becomes integral in reshaping the history while incorporating all its possibilities and complexities that existed in the past:

> The use of memory, then, as a rhetorical strategy both facilitated the construction of a progressive, black, historical subject and provided a bridge that connected degraded blacks to an illustrious past. This transhistorical subject could then be depicted as free to choose the historical path of resistance, so cherished by the ancestors, or remain in the degraded unnatural state of white domination. . . . Black nationalists used "black memory" to contest "white memory" and thus to create an American history with scope for blacks. (Gordon 182)

Blacks' celebration and glorification of African past, thus, besides being a form of resistance and a strategy for survival leads to positive memories for the present and the future generations.

Language, Form and Structure

Another significant aspect in cultural memory is language, as the deep-seated emotions and feelings lead to an emotional message which works as a vital insight to be passed on from generation to generation. The use of language can be seen as a connection between the African and the African American past and present. Demonstrating the significance of language, hooks affirms that the language has the ability to construct and deconstruct communities. Manner of speaking and dialect have a significant impact on an individual's identity. Language has repeatedly been employed to represent characters:

> To conceive an independent national identity, post-colonial writers concentrated on developing a symbolic vocabulary that was recognizably indigenous—or at least other to European representation. (Boehmer 178-79)

Lorraine Hansberry preferred the standard conventional form for writing her plays. Though her format was somehow similar to her white counterparts, she gave a special place to African culture in her works:

> She wished to combine the best of the West with the best of African culture . . . All of her plays use classic European dramatic forms, while often incorporating elements of the cultures of the diaspora from Africa, America, and the Caribbean. (Carter 16)

Lorraine Hansberry has used many African terminologies in her plays to add significance to the African culture. Asagai calls Beneatha with a Nigerian name, "Alaiyo." Asagai says, ". . . . It is a Yoruba word. I am a Yoruba" (65). Asagai, then tells Beneatha that Alaiyo means the one for whom bread and food is not enough. Beneatha thanks Asagai for the nickname as she understands that it represents her aspirations for achieving her dreams and not settling just for the basic needs. The terms OCOMOGOSIAY and OWIMOWEH were repeatedly used in act 2, scene 1. Hansberry also included a Yoruban song (Alundi, alundi) in her play which beautifully resonates as a signifier of her African heritage. Hansberry extensively made use of the dialect spoken by the black community. The characters in her play *A Raisin in the Sun*, use 'ain't' instead of haven't, wasn't and isn't, which reflects their inclination towards the African vernacular. For example, Walter tells Ruth, "Its been rough, ain't it baby" (88).

Beneatha gets an opportunity to go to college, therefore her language is a bit different, "Her speech is a mixture of many things; it is different from the rest of the family insofar as education has permeated her sense of English. . . . " (35). Thus, Hansberry's drama showcases diverse speech patterns of African American speech through her characters:

> In presenting the differing speech patterns of Mrs. Johnson, Walter, Beneatha, and even George Murchison, Hansberry affirms the validity of all and the fact that all are legitimate parts of African-American culture and have helped to enrich it. (Carter 27)

Suzan-Lori Parks can be easily differentiated from other playwrights as her theatre is very different from that of her predecessors. She invents her own rules, be it her language, style or spellings. She uses poetic and popular forms of speeches—word play, puns etc. Parks promotes fluidity in language and heterogeneity in vernacular dialect. She is noted for her non-traditional way of writing and its musical sense. Parks' drama also shows the influence of Greek writers as she uses chorus to introduce as well as comment on the present and future events. Chorus in her plays serves as a connection with the audiences:

> The Greek amphitheatre was the place where the community gathered not only to watch itself but also to reaffirm its superiority over others. Audiences participated as spectators and vicariously (thanks to the chorus), as performers within performance events that intended to

> create a sense of civic pride by staging the community's own prejudices as entertainment. (Young 45)

Parks' plays entail the interaction of ritual, memory, gender, history and language. She invents a new and a different stage language. She makes use of unconventional spellings, while her characters manipulate the language and speak African American vernacular. "It becomes the language of the fragmented, the dispossessed, the disjointed" (Kolin 16). Through the medium of language, Suzan-Lori Parks depicts her characters' insecurities, limitations and their search for some unity. In an interview with director Bonnie Metzgar, Parks says, "The language of the play should come from people's gut—what they want, what they don't want, what they're going through . . . what they are thinking" (qtd. in Kolin 48). In *Imperceptible Mutabilities in the Third Kingdom*, part 1: "Snails," Parks questions the biased conceptions pertaining to the black/white vernacular. Molly was expelled from school as she was not able to pronounce 'ask' correctly. Later in her workplace, she faces the same experience because of her way of speaking. Molly shares her experience with Charlene: "S-K" is /sk/ as in "ask. . . . Shit. Failed every test he shoves in my face. He makes me recite my mind goes blank" (25). This kind of treatment of Molly depicts that the black vernacular is considered as an unwelcome form, which is least acceptable in the American communities. Parks here refers to the Black English and its supposed inadequacy in mainstream America.

Language becomes a force in Parks' writing as it is linked to history. Parks employs a different vernacular dialect reverberating with the African American speech. In her plays, *The Death of the Last Black Man in the Whole Entire World*, *Venus* and *Fucking A*, she employs language fluidity. She doesn't confine herself to the African American vernacular. Parks' use of a peculiar language, based on African American vernacular is a way to resist the dominance of European discourse and to empower Blacks' vernacular. In *The Death of the Last Black Man in the Whole Entire World*, the characters use the altered spellings instead of the formal ones. As they spell 'round' as 'roun', thus deliberately obliterating the letter'd':

> BLACK MAN WITH WATERMELON: When thuhworlusta be roun.worlusta be roun.
>
> BLACK WOMEN WITH FRIED DRUMSTICK: Uh rounworl. Uh roun? Thuhworl? When was this?
>
> . . . .
>
> QUEEN-THE-PHARAOH HATSHEPSUT: Before Columbus thuhworlusta be roun they put /d/ on thuh end of round. Without that /d/ we coulda gone on spinnin forever. Thuh /d/ thing ended things ended. (102)

The preference of the Blacks for their own expressions is a form of resistance against the American English imposed by the Whites. Discarding standard English, Parks appropriates and subverts the Whites' language rejecting the conventional spellings, syntax, grammar and pronunciation. As Kolin puts it, "Inventing a new stage language, Parks has her characters speak an African American vernacular –a street-smart, rap like at times . . . which she records in phonetic and subversively unconventional spellings" (Kolin 16).

In *Death of the Last Black Man in the Whole Entire World*, Parks alters spellings in order to create varying interpretations. The Black Man's words are disorganised as he tries to find his place:

> We sittin on this porch right now aint we. Uh huhn. Yes. Sittin right here right now on it in aintthuh first time either iduhnt it Yep. Nope. Once we was here once wuhduhnt we . . . .Thuh. Then that was-be is uh has-been-Then too. Thuh me- has-been sits in thuh be-me: we sit on this porch. Same porch. Same me. (126)

About Parks' use of pun in abundance, Philip C. Kolin declares, "Thanks to her polyvalent, multidirectional puns, we travel over many miles and years, seeing and hearing suppressed black memories. We hear the bones sing, and wail" (Kolin 48).

The atrocities like inhuman treatment and lynching of Blacks are very poignantly portrayed by Parks in her plays. Among which one of the most horrible instances is rendered in the play, *The Death of the Last Black Man in the Whole Entire World*, where the Black Man is tormented by the white society and lynched. While articulating his experience, he expresses the manifestation of violence and oppression Blacks have to endure, "When I dieded they cut me down. Didnt have no need for me no more. They let me go. . . . Pulled me out of thuh trees then treed me then tired of me. That's how it has gone. Thatshow it be wentin" (119).

The play powerfully refers to the era of slavery. It reveals that the atrocities of the past persist even now. Through Black Man's repeated deaths, Parks reveals the violent assaults that Blacks endured during slavery. Parks employs a language easy to understand but powerful enough to have an unsettling effect on the reader. The words depict how Blacks were first cut off from their family trees, then enslaved and lynched. The Black Man with Watermelon appears on the stage carrying a tree branch with a piece of rope tied to his neck. When Black Man's wife asks him to remove the tree branch, "Somethin still holdin. Let me loosen your collar. . . . that now you can breathe you" (118). Black Man refuses as he wants to conserve it and says, "Don't take it off just loosen it. Don't move thuh tree branch let the tree branch be" (118). The branch of the tree symbolizes a part of Black Man's identity and heritage which he doesn't want to shake off. Besides that, the conversation between the Black Man and the Black Women throws light on the oppressed state of African Americans. "Through her repetitive, performative language, her puns, Parks re-enacts on stage the violence done to black bodies over time, thus inscribing their 'innard' history of oppression, but also their opposition to such indignities" (Kolin 48).

In an interview to Shawn-Marie Garret, Parks comments: "Writing used to mean just 'writing' but now maybe writing can include RIGHTING. Get right. Be right. Right. Write. Write on. Right on" (qtd. in Garret 185).

Parks challenges the traditional structure and form of writing which dominated the American theatrical landscape for long. She uses the unconventional technique of rep. and rev. "In the revisionary experience, African American identity looks on an image of being at once external and internal to itself, an echo or expression it must revise in order to see itself" (Larson 5). In *Venus*, Parks repeats and revises the historical moments. She deploys three chorus groups to proclaim certain events with slight modification each time.

In her play *Fucking A*, Parks creates and invents a language, 'TALK' which is used only by the women in the play. While strengthening the bond between women irrespective of race and class, it becomes a language of privacy as it is utilized by women when they communicate about their feminine or personal problems and throws light on the oppression of white women as well as black women.

Parks also employs spells in her plays which are defined by 'rests.' Parks writes, "This is a place where the figures experience their pure true simple state. . . . A spell is a place of great (unspoken) emotion. It's also a place for an emotional transition" (16-17). The character takes a break or rest in between their speech. Use of spells and rest makes her plays transformative. It takes a pause, little time to make transition. An appropriate usage of spell is seen in the play *FuckingA*, when Monster begs his mother to kill him before Hunters capture him but Hester is uncertain as her dream had been to liberate her son from prison:

> Hester
>
> Monster
>
> Hester
>
> Monster
>
> Hester. (219)

Shawn-Marie Garret writes, "Parks' spells move toward illuminations, not through . . . ecstatic shedding of the self, but through incantatory repetition that connects the individual to the great beyond: the past" (qtd. in Wetmore Jr & Howard 10). The spell is also depicted in her play, *In the Blood*, when Jabber repeats the word 'Slut' over and over again and hurts his mother's sentiments:

> Jabber: Slut. Sorry.
>
> Hester
>
> Jabber

Hester

Jabber. (105)

Parks and Hansberry hail from the new generation of playwrights who emerged and continued to expand the canon of African American Drama. They were influenced by Black Arts Movement, a movement which created a powerful black identity. Baraka notes: "It is Lorraine Hansberry's play which, though it seems "conservative" in form and content to the radical petty bourgeoisie . . . is the accurate telling and stunning vision of the real struggle" (qtd. in Elam, Jr. and Krasner 42).

Hansberry's plays are categorised as realistic plays with coherent plot, good characterisation and colloquial language. She emphasises realism but without any boundaries whatsoever. As she told Studs Terkel, "I think that imagination has no bounds in realism—you can do anything which is permissible in terms of the truth of the characters" (qtd. in Carter 190). Hansberry addresses social issues and impasse in her plays in the best possible manner. She expresses the challenging truths about Blacks through her characters. The play, *A Raisin in the Sun* unfolds the saga of the struggle of the Younger family to fulfil their dreams in the racist world of 1950s America and the ways how those dreams are deferred by a racist, classist and sexist society that the Younger family reside in. She challenges the controversial issues like women subordinacy, abortion, racism and gender roles of women and men. Baraka describes *A Raisin in the Sun* as a classic and further suggests, "it represents the "class and ideological struggles" of its time and "still remains overwhelmingly popular and evocative of black and white reality" (qtd. in Hannah 155).

Contrary to Hansberry, Parks elicits a distinct dramaturgy, nonlinear progressions, filtered language, archetypal characters, and abstract settings, fragmented structures and is more symbolic rather than realistic. She challenges the traditional narrative/ technique of representation of Blacks and women by questioning the intersection of multiple oppressions. Parks' use of nonlinear narratives and non-Standard English mirrors her individual vision which is framed by Blacks' and women's liberation movements. Parks writes, "I am working to create a dramatic text that departs from the traditional linear narrative style to look and sound more like a musical score" (9). Parks makes it clear in her essay, "From Elements of Style," that she is interested in exploring new things and forms, making her plays specific and unique in examination in contrast to general and easy interprctation.

Black Aesthetics

> As there is no single "Black Experience," there is no single "Black Aesthetic" and there is no one way to write or think or feel or dream or interpret or be interpreted. As African-Americans we should recognize this insidious essentialism for what it is: a fucked-up trap to reduce us to only one way of being. We should endeavour to show the world and ourselves our beautiful and powerfully infinitive variety. (Parks 21-22)

Parks' major focus lies in cultivating new ways for African Americans to form their identity, leaving aside the conventional way of confining their presence into the ideas of essential blackness and oppression. She challenges the traditional method of presenting Blacks' lives and moves way beyond the expectations of the audience from black artists and their works.

Parks uses postmodern techniques to transform the conventional forms of playwriting. Parks confronts the dominant ideologies which tend to subjugate Blacks. Andrea J. Goto explains in her essay "Digging Out of the Pigeonhole: African-American representation in the plays of Suzan-Lori Parks":

> Reversing or revising ideas such as 'whiteness' and 'blackness,' 'truth' and 'fiction,' or the ever-confounding notion of an 'American Identity,' the playwright treats them as malleable, dynamic concepts rather than a fixed ones, thus exposing the layers that compose an African-American identity and challenging her audiences to rethink racist assumptions and in its place see the human experience. (107-08)

In *Death of the Last Man in the Whole Entire World,* Parks seeks to deconstruct the stereotype of the Black Man associated with Watermelon and denies it to be the actual representation of a Black, depicting it as an utter absurdity. Parks adds that the racial stereotypes work as a hurdle for Blacks in expressing their identities.

Black Aesthetics rejected art for art's sake and focused on the political and social role of art. As a result of flux in Ku Klux Klan, majority of African American writers of the period realised the requisite to bring to the forefront the actual conditions of African Americans through their writing. In "Criteria for Negro Art" (1926), W.E.B. Du Bois asserts that his own writing "has been used always for propaganda for gaining the right of black folk to love and enjoy" (qtd. in *Odlum* 38).

The black writers bring to the forefront issues like racism, black identity, segregation, classism, and many such issues that have led to injustice to the Blacks. These writers believed that their writing has the power to ameliorate the stature of their people, although many African American writers during the 1950s digressed from writing "protest" literature in hope of integration and better relations between Whites and Blacks.

In Lorraine Hansberry's works protest is implied, however artfully disguised. She managed to work out an arrangement between the plans for integration which was in favour of Whites and those for Blacks' Pride ingrained in African American culture. Margaret B. Wilkerson argues about Hansberry's simultaneous particularism and universalism:

> She can write authentically about a black family in *A Raisin in thc Sun* and yet produce, in the same instance, a play which appeals to both Blacks and whites, bridging for a moment the historical and cultural gaps between them. (qtd. in Bernstein 98)

Lorraine Hansberry's *A Raisin in the Sun* depicts the plight of African Americans who were struggling hard during the time of integration. The play reveals the significance of the incorporation of a Black Aesthetics in countering racism in the United States. Though initially, the play was criticized for ignoring the values of Blacks but later it was realized by the black audience that the play deals with the interracial issues and identity which hold significance for Blacks. Hansberry has audaciously created an African American family who, despite their struggles, combat racism and classism collectively. In his essay "The Black Arts Movement" (1968), Larry Neal, one of the prominent voices of this movement, discusses the "new" Black Aesthetic: "In addition to art speaking directly to the African American community, participants within this movement would create a "radical reordering of the western cultural aesthetic" (qtd. in Odlum 39).

While employing blues, Jazz, African vernacular, dreams, history, both the playwrights connect to the past. The importance of the blues lies not only in its connection to music but in its relationship to history. By using blues, black writers have endeavoured to recapture the core of black culture and in a way glorified the beauty and strength of Blacks.

African American music and particularly jazz is employed in African American Literature. Jazz is a musical tone which is followed by repetition but with a slight change. This process is significant to the black vernacular. It erodes the false or distorted images about Blacks created by Whites and expresses the actual black experience. Leroi Jones, in his essay:

> The Myth of a Negro Literature," claims, "Only in music, and most notably in blues, jazz, and spirituals, i.e., "Negro Music,' has there been a significantly profound contribution {to American culture} by American Negroes. (qtd in Garret 286)

He aptly identifies that Negro music comes directly from the soul of Blacks. Jazz in a way restores the historical moment by recreating the silenced Black history:

> . . . the jazz musician and, later, the jazz writer adopted this new musical idiom predicated on African rhythms, ethnically specific practices of improvisation, black folk language, local urban themes, and the lives of ordinary black people as self -validating substitutes for the Eurocentric literary language, forms, subjects, and themes by which literary value has been determined. (Garret 287)

Parks' works rest upon the jazz aesthetic of "repetition and revision" through which Parks retrieves the old tradition connected with African American culture—songs, blues and jazz, thus utilising all the three forms for the representation of black history. The history of Jazz expands from the 19th century to the present and its etymology is as mysterious as that of the blues and many interpretations have been made about its origin. The impulse of jazz is full of vigour.

Blues music is primarily associated with traditional slave work songs and Negro spirituals. Mostly the early forms of black music take on the component of call and response. Blues exemplify the modern African American experience, depicting the hardships of slavery, great migration, cultural enthrallment and of procuring a secure space within the American society.

Jazz has the power to encourage Blacks to celebrate and articulate black identity amid racism and inequality. In Parks' play, *The Death of the Last Black Man in the Whole Entire World*, there is a refrain, "The black man moves his hands." It is repeated many times but with each repetition, there is a variation in gestures. It depicts the point of view and observation of the other characters in the play and the audience, who are all watching his actions. It further grants an opportunity for all to interpret it accordingly. In *Venus*, another such instance of repetition with slight revision is visible when The Brother, Later The Mother-Showman says, "Tail end of r tale for there must be an end / is that Venus . . . she sinned or else/completely unknowing of r godfearin ways she stood totally naked in her iron cage" (13). The same lines were repeated in the end by Venus but with a bit of modification: "Tail end of the tale for there must be uh end/ is that Venus. . . . completely unknowing thuhGodfearin ways, she stood/ Showing off her ass in her iron cage"(162).Venus authoritatively changes "r" to "thuh" and professes her distinctiveness in the end of the play which depicts that she has become habituated to her plight and finds agency within her own situation.

The spirituals, slavery songs and work songs are integral to slave culture and set foundation for jazz, blues and rock and roll. Loraine Hansberry employs African- American music to highlight Blacks' identity. She believes jazz, blues and other aspects of African-American culture as the most powerful ways of conveying the expression of freedom and identity. She depicts African practices like chanting, drumming and dancing in her plays.In her play, *To Be Young, Gifted and Black*, the love for blues, which African Americans consider their pride, is highlighted:

> How can I explain?
>
> But you
>
> Remind me of our blues. . .
>
> My blues—your blues—
>
> Ours. . . . (101)

In *A Raisin in the Sun*, the blues music is played within the play when Youngers were cleaning their house, "the radio is on and a Southside disk-jockey program is inappropriately filling the house with a rather exotic saxophone blues" (54). African American culture and music reinforces racial pride, the glimpse of which can be seen in their day-to-day life. Hansberry includes an African ceremonial dance in *A Raisin in the Sun* which refers to a racial pride and fondness between the brother and the sister. Beneatha plays a lovely Nigerian melody and performs a Nigerian folk dance, exclaiming, "OCOMOGOSIAY!". "Beneatha listens, enraptured, her eyes far away— back to the past" (77). She tells Ruth the significance of folk dance:

> Ruth: What kind of folks do that, honey?
>
> Beneatha: It's from Nigeria. It's a dance of welcome.
>
> Ruth: Who you welcoming?
>
> Beneatha: The men back to the village. . . .
>
> Beneath (With the record)
>
> Alundi, alundi. . . .
>
> Ang gusoooooooo. . . . (77)

The deep connection and intricate interrelationship of these characters with Africa is foregrounded in this scene. Then, Walter enters in a drunken state and joins his sister, shouting, "Me and Jomo . . . That's my man, Kenyatta. "FLAMING SPEAR HOT DAMN!" (78). Here Walter refers to the legendary African leader who bagged his freedom in 1959 after seven years of his trial for leading the Mau Mau rebellion against the colonial British rule of Kenya. Walter suddenly pulls his shirt open, leaps on the table, and pretends to hold a spear, shouting, "THE LION IS WAKING," symbolizing the assertion by Blacks for their freedom from colonial white rule. He tries to reacquire the lost African past through African tribal dance: 'OH, DO YOU HEAR, MY BLACK BROTHERS!' Margaret B. Wilkerson says, "Walter as signaling the wave of the future. He is restless, hungry, angry—a victim of his circumstance but at the same time the descendant of his proud forebears, struggling to transcend his victimhood" (qtd. in Bloom 35). Though both Beneatha and Walter are, in a sense, alienated from Africa, they attempt to relive their African-ness and proclaim it as part of their selfhood through the tribal dance.

In *Les Blancs*, Hansberry employs African music to showcase numerous facets of the play. For example the sound of the African drums at the onset of the play, "The sounds of bush grow louder. . . . we hear drums. . . . These are not all traditional 'movie drums' but distinct, erratic and varied statements of mood and intent" (41). Drum symbolises retaliation and resistance against oppression. Hansberry also brings in many images which are quintessentially African, images from the milieu that is inseparable from their sensibility: the sounds from the jungle e.g. sounds of crickets, frogs, bush babies, cry of birds and laughter of a hyena. These sounds envisage the African twilight.

Also, an African woman dancer is introduced in the prologue whose persona represents Africa. The enchanting woman signifies the slaughter and enslavement:

> A WOMAN, majestic and motionless, appears. Black-skinned and imposing, cheeks painted for war. . . . From her wrists and ankles hang bangles of feathers and silver. . . . She advances slowly majestically, to mounting drumbeats, in an unmistakable dance of the warriors. (41)

The play reflects upon the customs and practices of Africa where drumbeating is a ritual signifying war or death.

In her posthumous play *To Be Young, Gifted, and Black*, in part 1, section 5 titled "Of Vikings and Congo Drums" Hansberry describes her character Candace:

> One thing was certain: she was at one texture, blood, follicles of hair, nerve ends, all with the sound of a mighty Congo drum. She had never heard African music that had

> not set her mad with romance of her people, never. . . . her heart rose in her bossom, her teeth set, her eyes widened, and Africa claimed her. . . . (75)

The sound of the African drum seems to bring Candace into consciousness. Hansberry shows in her letters and memoirs, integrated into the autobiographical text, *To Be Young, Gifted, and Black*, a similar feeling of being captivated by Africa as a dreamland and as an escape from the harsh realities of American society.

In the play, *The Drinking Gourd*, Hansberry incorporates many slave songs. The slaves recite songs/poems like "The Drinking Gourd," "Steel Away," and many more. All these songs reflect the state of mind, emotions and actions of slaves. In act 2, slaves sing a song, "Raise a Ruckus, depicting the evil of slavery and at the same time mocking their masters:

> Joshua: My old master promised me. . . .
>
> That when he died he gona set me free. . . .
>
> Then he gave up the notion of dying at all!
>
> All:. . . .
>
> We're gona raise a ruckus tonight!
>
> Sarah: My old mistress promise me.
>
> MmmMmm . . . (Mimicking)
>
> "Say-rah! When I die I'm going to set you free!
>
> MmmMmmMmm
>
> But a dose of poison kinda helped her along
>
> MmmMmmMmm

And may the devil sing her funeral song! (197)

Slaves become aware of the fact that they are not secure and decide to run away to attain their freedom. When there is little action, songs become the powerful medium of expression with myriad connotations in Hansberry's plays.

Similarly, Parks is also known for incorporating songs, chorus and music in her plays to express the plight and feelings of her characters. Music in a way symbolises Parks' own creative life. In an interview, she tells Garret about writing songs, " . . . All my writing is more like songs, cause in a song you're in the ocean, the ocean of emotion . . . that's what it feels like, trying to write . . . I try to sing to people" (qtd. in Garret 189). In her play *Father Comes Home from the Wars*, Hansberry uses many songs which provide an in-depth understanding of the situation and are utilized to comment on the action taking place. In part-3, "The Union of My Confederate Parts," there is a song titled "Misplaced Myself" which depicts about the runaway slaves: ". . . . I'm long gone/ I ain't minding in your store/ . . . You don't matter anymore. . . . I have misplaced myself" (107). These lines also refer to the historical period when African American slaves escaped from the clutches of their owners. Music, therefore, becomes a way of resistance in the face of trauma. It also becomes a source of bonding between Blacks.

Intertextuality

Literature communicates history and culture by reincorporating the suppressed traditions, incidents, stories that have become a part of collective memory. The term Intertextuality was coined by Julia Kristeva in 1966 to denote the interdependence of literary texts, "the interdependence of any one literary text with all those that have gone before it" (Cuddon 424). Intertextuality refers to a conscious attempt to incorporate the elements of one text such as the technique, form, story, genre, etc. into another. It can be seen as an interrelation between different texts but contributes to a fresh comprehension of the new text which incorporates the elements of the old text. Lachmann's observation clearly highlights the way it redefines the book culture:

> Intertextuality demonstrates the process by which a culture, where "culture" is a book culture, continually rewrites and retranscribes itself, constantly redefining itself through its signs. Every concrete text, as a sketched-out memory space, connotes the macrospace of memory that either represents a culture or appears as that culture. (301)

Parks employs the device of intertextuality in her plays in order to convey the saga of oppression of African Americans as well as to interrogate the stereotypes associated with the Blacks. She showcases through her plays the revised or recreated texts and contexts related to Blacks, culture and history.

Parks employs several intertextual references in her plays from both her own as well as others' works. Her *Red Letter Plays*: *In the Blood* and *Fucking A* are based on Nathaniel Hawthorne's 1850 novel *The Scarlet Letter.* In an interview with Kevin. J. Wetmore, Jr., Parks tells about how she decided to write the play *Fucking A:*

> With *Fucking A*, I was in a canoe with a friend . . . 'I'm going to write a play called *Fucking A*, and its going to be riff on *The Scarlet Letter*. . . . I hadn't actually read *The Scarlet Letter*. . . . So then I had to read *The Scarlet Letter.*

> Then figure out what about *The Scarlet Letter* had so sneakily hooked me. (qtd. in Wetmore, Jr 124)

Hester of Nathaniel Hawthorne's *The Scarlet Letter* was treated as an outcast by being forced to bear the mark of the letter 'A' for her act of indulging in adultery. Similarly in Parks' play *In the Blood*, the central character who shares the same name, Hester, is depicted as an outcast because she has begotten five children out of wedlock. Like Hester Prynne, Parks' Hester in *Fucking A*, wears the Letter A above her left breast. This 'A' is branded into her which she does not want anybody to see:

> Hester: I don't like people staring.
>
> Butcher: Why do they brand you aborters?. . . .
>
> Hester: The brand come with the job. . . "And the brand must be visible all the times." Thats the law. (164)

It signifies the oppression, injustice and exploitation of black woman who is branded as an abortionist. It also highlights patriarchal domination. Parks uses the story of Hester in *The Scarlet Letter* with a bit of variation and thus depicts the agony of the African American woman. She showcases her sad plight and an oppressive situation because she is Black. She suffers more in comparison to the White Hester of *The Scarlet Letter*. "Hester Prynne's oppression is certainly real and relevant, Hester La Negrita's, two centuries later, is not only deeper, but also more pervasive" (Larson 43). Intertextuality has been used by Parks' in *Topdog/ Underdog, The America Play, In the Blood* and *Fucking A*. In *Topdog/ Underdog* and *The America Play*, Parks casts black impersonators of Abraham Lincoln who struggle for their identity. In both the plays, characters with same names, Lincoln, impersonate the President Abraham Lincoln and enact his assassination in order to earn a living. Both the characters wear makeup, costumes and masks so as to pass for the Whites and hide their actual identity as they wanted to be recognized and accepted in the white world. Parks refers to the painful history of the Blacks' suffering in their day-to-day lives. "In both plays these shooters sanction their desire to participate in historical re-creation . . . shifting Lincoln-the-President's identity onto The Foundling Father and Lincoln himself" (Larson 68).

Likewise, there are many similarities in Parks' *Red Letter Plays* which include *In the Blood* and *Fucking A*. In both the plays mothers have no support from society but endeavour to fit in the conventional model of good matriarch. Parks represents dual images of a mother: nurturing and murderous in both the plays. They symbolize all those suffering black women who break down and end up destroying their family and themselves. It would not be wrong to say that both the characters are created and later destroyed by their own world and society. Verna Foster rightfully points out, "the two Hesters ultimately harm those they love and themselves "without effecting any change in the social conditions that produced their rages" (qtd. in Dietrick101). *The Red Letter plays* also emphasize the importance of literacy, since they draw on the possibilities for self- affirmation as well as expression. In *Fucking A*, Scribe throws light on the importance of education and says, "Dad wanted me to make something of myself. So he stood over me with a stick. . . . Perfectly formed letter at 3 years old" (140). There are many people in their community who are not able to write. Scribe writes for them. Hester also asks Scribe to write a letter to her son in prison. She praises his writing and says, "He makes the nicest looking letters. Even when hes sloshed. Such pretty shapes, straight bold lines and gentle curls. Makes me wish I could read. And write too" (159). Hester in *In the Blood,* adamantly declares to Amiga Gringa, "I can write my damn name. Im not such a fool that I cant write my own goddamn name. I can write my goddamn name" (32). Though she can write only one letter, 'A,' through which she seems to express her emotional anxiety. Larson rightly says:

> If Hester can indeed read and write, then the obvious limits on her literacy—the forces that make some letters mysterious –must come from circumstance. Hester's longing for self-expression compels her to demonstrate this literacy in particular ways to fit particular situations and leads her to focus on the letter A because of its relevance to her. (46)

In an interview with Kevin J. Wetmore, Parks talks about interconnectedness of all things in her plays:

> KJW: There's such a sense of the interconnectedness of things in your plays . . .
>
> SLP: Wow. That's a play in 365. *The Interconnectedness of All Things.*
>
> KJW: . . . . You talk about 'rev &rep' but I would add a third: 'ref.' It's not just revision and repetition, but also reference.
>
> SLP: Oohh, that's good! 'Rev and rep and ref.' (qtd. in Wetmore, Jr 129 30)

Then, there is an intertextual reference within the play *Venus* also. Parks repeatedly uses the title, "For the love of Venus" in scenes 4, 8,11,23,26 and 29. Parks utilizes some scenes and lines from Tom Taylor's *Our American Cousin*, "On that stage that night was *Our American Cousin* starring Miss Laura Keene. The plot of the play is of little consequence to our story. . . . " (167). This was the play, Abraham Lincoln was watching when he was assassinated by John Wilkes Booth. Parks refers to the exact lines from acts of the play frequently in act 2: The Hall of Wonders in Echo section. Parks includes in her play, the most famous lines from Tom Taylor's *Our American Cousin*, "Don't know the manners of good society, eh? Wal, I guess I know enough to turn you inside out, old gal—you sockdologizing old man-trap" (188). When Mr. Trenchard, a character from *Our American Cousin* said these lines, Abraham Lincoln was shot dead by Booth.

Lorraine Hansberry also employs intertextuality in some of her plays. There are similarities between *Les Blancs* and Shakespeare's *Hamlet*. Both the plays are developed on the similar storyline where the protagonists have returned from abroad to attend the funeral of their fathers.

From the colonial perspective also, there is an analogy between *Les Blancs* and *Hamlet* as both the plays aimed at liberating their nations from injustice and tyranny of colonial powers:

> Hansberry emphasizes the full viciousness and insidiousness in the cooptation of some Africans, such as AbiosehMatoseh, into the colonial power structure by comparing this to Claudius's manipulation of Laertes into fighting on the side of his true enemy, Claudius himself, against a fellow victim, Hamlet. (Carter 102)

Another resemblance among the two plays is the use of supernatural powers. The action of the protagonists is prompted by the spirits. Initially both Hamlet and Tshembe are reluctant in taking an appropriate action. Carter notes:

> . . . the intellectual Tshembe is slow to commit himself and perform his duties. . . . And while Hamlet agonises over the immoral relationship his mother has with his stepfather, Tshembe perhaps grieves over the sex forced on his mother by Major Rice, Rice's supposed "rape" of her symbolizing the rape of an entire continent by white imperialists. (qtd. in Leeson 65)

The bond between the mother and the son is illustrated in both the plays. Though Madame Neilsen, who was a white woman, was not the actual mother of Tshembe, she was a motherly figure for Tshembe and was very dear to him. Hamlet and Tshembe are very close to their mothers.

Another striking parallel is visible in the ending of both the plays. The ending of the plays is tragic as many innocent people sacrifice their lives. As Mr. Clurman observes, "What the ending signifies is that mankind has always made its progress through a mess of bloody injustices and inevitable cruelty. . . ."(qtd. in Hansberry 134).

The title for Hansberry's play*A Raisin in the Sun*, makes an intertextual reference to a poem, "Harlem" also known as "A Dream Deferred" by the Harlem Renaissance poet Langston Hughes which was published in 1951 in his book *Montage of a Dream Deferred*. Both the texts address concerns pertaining to the Blacks' dreams and further depict the limited scope of fulfilling these dreams in America. There are many deferred dreams in *A Raisin in the Sun* also. All the characters have dreams waiting to be realized. The title of the play is also taken from the lines of this poem:

> What happens to a dream deferred?

Does it dry up

like a raisin in the sun?. . . .

Or does it explode? (qtd. in Hansberry 3)

The poem questions whether people surrender to circumstances of their lives or they strive hard to attain their dreams. Likewise, Hansberry examines how the dreams of black America have been ignored, deferred or achieved. The dreams of all the characters are considered as least significant by the white society and Blacks are forced to defer or give up their dreams. The play chronicles the struggle of each character to attain their dreams.

Intertextuality occurs in *The Drinking Gourd* also. The title of the play *The Drinking Gourd* is borrowed from a spiritual song, "Follow the Drinking Gourd," a song of Underground Railroad which reflects the freedom for the escaped slaves who want to make a way towards North. Hansberry has referred to the dreams of slaves for liberty and equality throughout the play. Just like his brother Isaiah who escaped to the North, Hannibal, the protagonist of the play expresses his dream to escape from this tyrannical world and slave system.

In *To Be Young, Gifted and Black*, Hansberry utilizes variety of her works as a point of reference. It is a play of theatrical and sentimental memories which are reflected through switching to her earlier plays and memories throughout the play. The text comprises fragments from her speeches, articles, transcripts of interviews, poetry, fiction and unpublished as well as published plays. Scenes from her plays are integrated together to form a composite whole.

Hansberry entrusted her husband as the literary executor of all her works that were started by her but were not completed. She says, "If anything should happen—before tis done—may I trust that all commas and periods will be placed and someone will complete my thoughts—This last should be the least difficult—since there are so many who think as I do—"(265).

Nemiroff took the assistance and help of many people who were associated with Hansberry to complete the play of the same name. Nemiroff took the title from a phrase, 'To be Young, Gifted and Black,' which is coined by Hansberry herself.

Lorraine Hansberry's and Suzan-Lori Parks' works are influenced by their personal lives and experiences. Both the writers have weaved their plays in accordance with what they have experienced as Black women.

Though Lorraine Hansberry and Suzan-Lori Parks belong to different periods, differ in their literary techniques, they played a dominant role in the evolution of presenting Black Aesthetics in a powerful way. They turn the mirror towards Blacks, showing self-awareness, authentic representation of Blacks in contrast to the negative stereotypes perpetuated by the Whites. Both the playwrights endeavoured and succeeded in interrogating the authenticity of the history crafted by the Whites by relocating the actual identity of Blacks through their works.

5
Authentic Black Voices

The two African American playwrights emerged as powerful spokespersons for the Blacks and Africanism. They articulate not just the unbearable agony undergone by their race but also their spirit of freedom. Portraying the tormented and the free spirit both, these writers deal with themes like racism, slavery, poverty as well as their empowered selves. As they endeavour to mark their presence in world literature, their portrayal of Blacks emerges to be different from the clichéd projections of their race made by the Whites. Glorifying the rich culture and history of Blacks by voicing their opinions through the characters in their plays, they encouraged Blacks to think critically to assert themselves by opposing their oppressors.

These playwrights question the supposed superiority of the Whites and in the light of postcolonial discourse, showcases Blacks' identity from a historical perspective and attempts to reconstruct their lived history by emphasising some significant facts and incidents which had been deliberately kept under wraps since ages. The plays of Hansberry and Parks unambiguously refer to some momentous events in Africa while highlighting the pertinent social and political issues. In numerous ways, they poignantly evoke the trauma and resistance of the Blacks. An unequal social order owing to racial prejudices is presented as a major hurdle in the way of African Americans who aspire to be as successful as their white counterparts.

Both Hansberry's and Parks' pride in their identity and origins and the scope of their vision are vital to their uncommon and revolutionary consciousness. They were aware of the prejudices that Blacks as well as the Whites harboured and also knew that they are the larger issues that are more important and must be confronted. They believed in challenging the social order that held Blacks in subjugation even after slavery had been officially abolished.

Lorraine Hansberry and Suzan-Lori Parks endeavoured to confront racism that resulted in acute oppression of the Black people. Their plays authentically mirror the system of slavery and its devastating effects reflecting their awareness of the realities of the historical period. They furnish a realistic portrayal of slavery and bring some harsh truths to the fore many of which would have remained unnoticed otherwise. The question vehemently raised by both the writers is the approach where Blacks are associated with negative traits while Whites are depicted with positive attributes. White superiority has traditionally been seen in sharp contrast to black inferiority by many. The persecution faced by the Blacks at the hands of the Whites due to the malaise of slavery showcases the relationship between the masters and the servants, who were treated with utter contempt.

The themes of bigotry, poverty and oppression are addressed by both the playwrights. Although they were born and brought up in material comfort, they were also subjected to discrimination that the Blacks in America were victims of. Both the authors always identified themselves with the poor black people and never isolated themselves from the struggle of poor blacks. Their plays foreground the actual suffering of Blacks while showcasing economic constraints and poverty of those living on the margin of society. Relegated to subservient jobs, the Blacks do not get equal opportunities in accordance with their capabilities unlike the Whites. Their dreams remain unfulfilled, which is a prominent theme in African American drama and is addressed by these two playwrights too. The great American dream emerges as a symbol of hope for freedom and equality on one hand and the frustration and alienation, particularly for the Blacks on the other. The economic hardships, lack of job opportunities and all-pervasive inequities of society restrict the growth of the Blacks living on the margin of society.

Hansberry and Parks weave their personal experiences in some of their plays which give them an autobiographical touch; however, their plays are not overtly first-person accounts. In fact, their personal traumas are a reflection of the lives of the fellow Blacks. The stark truth and painful reality of racism is unequivocally expressed in their plays. Hansberry had some painful experiences in life that had a deep impact on her psyche. The picture of ghetto life that she paints can very well be attributed to this fact. She developed a sense of sympathy, concern, affection and understanding towards the oppressed people of her community whom she portrays in her plays authentically and invests them with dignity.

The social and historical backdrop of Hansberry's drama was formed by the momentous social and political events of 1950s and 1960s. She was powerfully drawn towards this scenario. The depth and breadth of Hansberry's social and political concerns are therefore clearly manifested in her works. She threw herself heart and soul into the conflicts and became by virtue of her public speeches a mighty voice among the Blacks:

> Hansberry took that naturalistic style and deliberately infused it with an array of ideas, which many other writers were consciously not doing. Beyond the message that Black is now real and good, there was no other dimension to the political and social concepts of Black drama. Hansberry was an intensely political person. (qtd. in Gomez 41)

With the underlying objective of bringing forth the interconnectedness of literature and history, the major focus of both the writers remained in foregrounding the significance of historical and cultural events through their literary masterpieces. Cultural and historical memories are vital as the present and future are shaped by the recollection of past memories. "Occasionally, there are historical memories that are so overwhelmingly significant that they define the essence of a people and become imperative for their survival" (Rodríguez and Fortier 11). Hansberry and Parks incorporate the historical past and memories of the African Americans in their plays, highlighting their struggle to attain freedom from the clutches of slavery. Besides, they also showcase the glorious and rich African heritage.

Although both the playwrights' choice of themes makes their drama, a drama about the Black struggle for liberation, they also espouse some universal themes in the plays like assertion, women's rights, the American Dream, man-woman relationship and so on. Hansberry and Parks always had a profound reverence for womanhood. They express through their plays, a deep sensitivity towards the complexities of women's lives under challenging and difficult situations. Their women characters are very dignified and inherently strong. They have powerful attributes like the spirit of sacrifice and endurance.

Hansberry and Parks deal with the oppression faced by the black women and their double marginalization. The portrayal of their characters Beneatha, Ruth, Hester and Venus convey that women suffer dual oppression in a male dominated racist society. Hansberry's recognition of her blackness and femaleness was the starting point for her philosophical journey from the Chicago to the world community.

The American theatre and the African American theatre owe so much to Lorraine Hansberry that her contribution cannot be belittled. Aside from the pleasure of reading, the works of Hansberry have one definite object, and that is to acquaint her readers and audiences with reality. Her fellow writer James Baldwin noted in the introduction to Hansberry's autobiography:

> I had never in my life seen so many black people in the theatre, and the reason was that never before, in the entire history of the American theatre, had so much of truth of black people's lives been seen on the stage. (qtd.in Leeson 19)

She was a master of heightened realism. Her search was always for the uniqueness, the extraordinary in the ordinary which she reflected through the characters in her plays. The heroes of her plays are the ordinary people. She wished to reach the general theatre audience. Amiri Baraka celebrates *A Raisin in the Sun* as a work of critical realism that moves beyond mere realism in its most limited form. That is, Hansberry "analyzes and assesses reality and shapes her statement as an aesthetically powerful and politically advanced work of art" (qtd.in Leeson 151). "Hewes appreciated *A Raisin in the Sun*'s being about "real people" who only happen to be "colored people," noting their "inner family joys and anxieties[as] universal ones" (qtd. in Leeson 31).

Hansberry and Parks depict their characters not only as victims but also strong figures who assert their identity. They not only articulate their experiences of atrocities and horrors perpetrated on them very strongly but firmly proclaim their identity with all their vices and goodness. The journey of transformation from suppression to assertion is clearly depicted through their characters who retaliate against the hegemony of Whites' and Males' ideals and dominance.

Both the playwrights sought to create an authentic black voice. Their protagonists are portrayed as strong willed and assertive figures who voice their views against the dominant white constructs. They were capable enough to create characters who lived and grew. They have the strength of spirit, will and mind—traits which reflect the powerful personas of both the authors. The characters like Lena, Rissa and Hannibal in Hansberry's plays and Hester, Venus, Black man with Watermelon and Arthea in Parks' plays reflect the power to assert in hostile surroundings.

Hansberry's and Parks' contribution as African American women writers and also as social activists is outstanding. Their oeuvre continues to influence and encourage younger generations. In all their works, whether opposing the slave trade, or pleading for justice for African Americans or protecting women in a male dominated society, Hansberry and Parks aimed solely at social justice. Embittered by the treatment of the Blacks by the Whites, their personal awareness about the conditions of the poor black people and their families' dedication and commitment towards eradication of injustice and prejudice emerged as powerful social statements in their drama.

Hansberry and Parks created a tradition by reconstructing the past laying bare all its hidden recesses so that the future generations would value and preserve their own culture and history. Their observations and vision embody a remarkable foresight and relevance making their drama truly worthy of universal appreciation.

Bibliography

1. Primary Sources

Hansberry, Lorraine. *Les Blancs*. *Les Blancs: The Collected Last Plays*. Edited by Robert Nemiroff. Vintage Books, 1972, pp. 37-128.

---. *The Drinking Gourd.Les Blancs: The Collected Last Plays*. Edited by Robert Nemiroff. Vintage Books, 1972, pp. 163-217.

---. *A Raisin in the Sun*. Vintage Books, 1988.

---.*To Be Young Gifted and Black*. Signet Classics,1969.

Parks, Suzan-Lori. *The America Play. The America Play and Other Works*. Theatre Communications Group, 1995, pp.157-99.

---. *Betting on the Dust Commander. The America Play and Other Works*. Theatre Communications Group, 1995, 73-90.

---. *The Death of the Last Black Man in the Whole Entire World. The America Play and OtherWorks*. Theatre Communications Group, 1995, pp. 99-132.

---. *Father Comes Home From The Wars*. Theatre Communication Group, 2015.

---. *Fucking A*. *The Red Letter Plays*. 1998. Theatre Communications Group, 2001, pp.1-112.

---. *Imperceptible Mutabilities in the Third Kingdom. The America Play and Other Works*. Theatre Communications Group, 1995, pp. 23-72.

---. *In the Blood. The Red Letter Plays*. Theatre Communications Group, 2001, pp. 113-225.

---. *Pickling. The America Play and Other Works*.Theatre Communications Group, 1995, pp. 91-98.

---.*Topdog/Underdog*. Dramatists Play Service, 2002.

---.*Venus*. Dramatists Play Service, 1995.

2. Secondary Sources

Abrams, M. H. *A Glossary of Literary Terms*, 7th ed. Harcourt Brace College Publishers, 1999.

Allen, Graham . *Intertextuality*. Routledge, 2000.

Anderson, Mary Louise. “Black Matriarchs Should Be Admired.”Wiener, pp. 139-146.

Ashcroft, Bill, et al. *Post Colonial Studies: The Key Concepts*, 2nd ed., Routledge, 2007.

Baraka, Amiri. *Digging: The Afro-American Soul of American Classical Music*. U of California P, 2009.

Barry, Peter. *Beginning Theory: An Introduction to Literary and Cultural Theory*. 2nd ed., Manchester UP, 2019.

Bassnett, Susan. *Comparative Literature: A Critical Introduction*. Blackwell, 1993.

Beaulieu, Elizabeth Ann, editor. *Writing African American Women: An Encyclopedia of Literature by and about Women of Color*. vol.1, Greenwood, 2006.

Behdad, Ali and Dominic Thomas, editors. *A Companion to Comparative Literature.* Wiley-Blackwell, 2011.

Berghahn, Marion. *Images of Africa in Black American Literature*. Macmillan Press, 1977.

Bernheimer, Charles, editor. *Comparative Literature in the Age of Multiculturalism*. Johns Hopkins UP, 1995.

Bernstein, Robin. "Robin Bernstein on the Play's Critical Reception." Bloom, pp. 91-100.

Bertens, Hans. *Literary Theory: The Basics*. Routledge, 2001.

Bhabha, Homi K. Foreword. *Black Skin, White Masks*, by Frantz Fanon, translated by Charles Lam Markmann, Pluto, 2008, pp. xxi-xxxvi.

Bloom, Harold, editor. *Lorraine Hansberry's a Raisin in the Sun*. Bloom's Literary Criticism, 2009.

---, Introduction. *Lorraine Hansberry's a Raisin in the Sun*, edited by Bloom. Bloom's Literary Criticism, 2009, pp. 7-8.

Boehmer, Elleke. *Colonial and Postcolonial Literature: Migrant Metaphors*. 2nd ed. Oxford UP, 2005.

Brannigan, John. *New Historicism and Cultural Materialism*. Macmillan Press, 1998.

Brewer,Rose M. "Theorizing race, class and gender: The new scholarshipof Black feminist intellectuals and Black women's labor." James and Busia, pp.13-30.

Brown, Janet. "Feminist theory and contemporary drama." Murphy. pp. 155-72.

Bruce Jr., Dickson D. *The Origins of African American Literature, 1680-1865*. UP of Virginia, 2001.

Burke, Sally. "Hansberry's Play Depicts Strong-Willed Women Who Refuse to Be Marginalized." Wiener, pp. 88-97.

Carter, Steven R. *Hansberry's Drama: Commitment Amid Complexity*. U of Illinois P, 1993.

---. "Beneatha Fights Male Chauvinism as well as Her Own Flaws."Wiener. pp. 98-105.

Collins, Patricia Hill. *Black Feminist Thought: Knowledge, Consciousness, and the Politics of Empowerment*. Routledge, 2002.

---. *From Black Power to Hip Hop: Racism, Nationalism, and Feminism*. Temple UP, 2006.

Cover copy. *Les Blancs: The Collected Last Plays*, by LorraineHansberry, edited by Robert Nemiroff. Vintage Books, 1972.

Cuddon, John Anthony. *A Dictionary of Literary Terms and Literary Theory*, revised by C.E. Preston, 4th ed., Blackwell, 1998.

Davidson, et al. editors. *Convergences: Black Feminism and Continental Philosophy*, Sunny Press, 2010.

Davies, Carole Boyce. *Black Women, Writing, and Identity: Migrations of the Subject*. Routledge, 1994.

Davis, Carol Bunch and Alexis M. Skinner."*A Raisin in the Sun*."Page, *Icons of African American Literature*, pp. 345-66.

Dietrick, Jon. "A Full Refund Aint Enough": Money in Suzan-Lori Parks's*Red Letter Plays*." Kolin, pp. 88-102.

Dixon, Kimberly D. "Uh Tiny Land Mass Just Outside of My Vocabulary: Expression of Creative Nomadism and Contemporary African American Playwrights."Elam and Krasner. pp. 212-34.

Elam, Harry J., and David Krasner. *African-American Performance and Theater History: A Critical Reader*. Oxford UP, 2001.

Erll, Astrid. "Cultural Memory Studies: An Introduction." Erll, and Nünning, pp. 1-18.

Erll, Astrid and Ansgar Nünning, editors. *Cultural Memory Studies: An International and Interdisciplinary Handbook*. Walter de Gruyter, 2008.

Fanon, Frantz. *Black Skin, White Masks*. Translated by Charles Lam Markmann. Pluto, 2008.

Fisch, Audrey A., editor. *The Cambridge Companion to the African American Slave Narrative*. Cambridge UP , 2007.

Garret, Shawn-Marie Garrett. " An interview with Suzan-Lori Parks."Kolin, pp. 181-90.

Goddard, Lynette. *Staging Black Feminisms: Identity, Politics, Performance*. Palgrave Macmillan, 2007.

Gold, Rachelle S. "'Education has spoiled many a good plow hand': How Beneatha's Knowledge Functions in A Raisin in the Sun." Harris and Larson, pp.1-20.

Gomez, Jewelle L. "Hansberry Is an Inspiration to Later Writers and Activists." Wiener, pp. 35-48.

Gordon, Dexter B. *Black Identity: Rhetoric, Ideology, and Nineteenth-Century Black Nationalism*. Southern Illinois UP, 2003.

Goto, Andrea J. "Digging Out of the Pigeonhole: African-American representation in the plays of Suzan-Lori Parks." Wetmore Jr., and Smith, pp. 106-23.

Guerin, Wilfred L. *A Handbook of Critical Approaches to Literature*. Oxford UP, 2011. Guillén, Claudio. *The Challenge of Comparative Literature*. Translated by Cola Franzen. Harvard UP, 1993.

Hannah, John M. "Signifying Raisin: Hansberry's *A Raisin in the Sun* and Wilson's *Fences*." Harris and Larson, pp. 153-82.

Harris, Trudier. "Mama Lena Is an Acceptable Tyrant." Wiener, pp. 114-29.

Harris, Trudier, and Jennifer Larson, editors. *Reading Contemporary African American Drama: Fragments of History, Fragments of Self*. Peter Lang, 2007.

Hartog, François. *The Mirror of Herodotus: The Representation of the Other in the Writing of History*. Translated by Janet Lloyd, U of California P, 2009.

Healey, Joseph F. *Race, Ethnicity, Gender, and Class: The Sociology of Group Conflict and Change*. Pine Forge Press, 2009.

hooks, bell. *Where We Stand: Class Matters*. Routledge, 2000.

---. *Ain't I a Woman: Black Women and Feminism*. Routledge, 2015.

Huskey, R. Erin. "Alice Walker."Page, *Icons of African American Literature*, pp. 447-70.

James, Stanlie M, and Abena P. A. Busia. *Theorizing Black Feminisms: The Visionary Pragmatism of Black Women*. Routledge, 1993.

Jarrett, Gene Andrew, editor. *A Companion to African American Literature*. Wiley-Blackwell, 2010.

Jarrett-Macauley, Delia. *Reconstructing Womanhood, Reconstructing Feminism: Writings on Black Women*. Routledge, 2005.

Kachur, Matthew, and Philip Schwarz. *The Slave Trade*. Chelsea House, 2006.

Kamli, Leila. *The Cultural Memory of African American and Black British Fiction: Specters of the Shore*, 1st ed., Palgrave Macmillan, 2016.

Kolin, Philip C., editor. *Suzan-Lori Parks: Essays on the Plays and Other Works*. McFarland, 2010.

Lachmann, Renate . "Mnemonic and Intertextual Aspects of Literature"ErllandNunning,pp. 301-10.

Larson, Jennifer. *Understanding Suzan-Lori Parks*. U of South Carolina P. 2012.

Leeson, Richard M. *Lorraine Hansberry: A Research and Production Sourcebook*. Greenwood Press, 1997.

Loomba, Ania. *Colonialism/Postcolonialism*. Routledge, 2000

Mafe Diana Adesola, "Diana Adesola Mafe on Hansberry and Ntozake Shange"Bloom, pp. 136-45.

Marshall, Annecka. "From sexual denigration to self-respect:resisting images of Black female sexuality." Jarrett-Macauley, pp. 5-36.

Marsico, Katie. *Slavery in America*. Rourke Educational Media, 2014.

Moore-Gilbert, Bart. *Postcolonial Theory: Contexts, Practices, Politics*. Verso, 2000.

Morrison, Toni. *Playing in the Dark: Whiteness and the Literary Imagination*. Vintage Books, 1992.

---. *The Source of Self-Regard: Selected Essays, Speeches, and Meditations*. Alfred A. Knopf, 2019.

Murphy, Brenda, editor. *The Cambridge Companion to American Women Playwrights*. Cambridge UP, 1999.

Nemiroff, Jewell Handy Gresham. Foreword. *Les Blancs. Les Blancs: The Collected Last Plays*,by Lorraine Hansberry, edited by Robert Nemiroff, Vintage Books, 1972, pp. xiii-xxi.

Nemiroff, Robert. Introduction. *A Raisin in the Sun*, by Lorraine Hansberry, Vintage Books, 1988, pp. 1-15.

Odlum, Lakisha. "Black Aesthetic."Page, *Icons of African American Literature*, pp. 35-42

Page, Yolanda Williams, editor. *Icons of African American Literature: The Black Literary World*. Greenwood, 2011.

Peach, Linden, editor. *New Casebooks: Toni Morrison*. Macmillan, 1998.

Parks, Suzan-Lori. "An Equation for Black People Onstage." *The America Play and Other Works*. Theatre Communications Group, 1995, pp. 19-22.

---. "From Elements of Style." *The America Play and Other Works*. Theatre Communications Group, 1995, pp. 6-18.

---. "Possession." *The America Play and Other Works*. Theatre Communications Group, 1995, pp. 3-5.

Parry, Benita. *Postcolonial Studies: A Materialist Critique*. Routledge, 2004.

Persley, Nicole Hodges. "Sampling and Remixing: Hip Hop and Parks's History Plays." Kolin., pp. 65-78.

Rodriguez, Jeanette, and Ted Fortier. *Cultural Memory: Resistance, Faith & Identity*. U of Texas P, 2007.

Rushdy, Asharaf H. A. "Daughters Signifyin(g) History: The Example of Toni Morrison's *Beloved*." Peach, pp. 140-53.

Russell, Lynette, editor. *Boundary Writing: An Exploration of Race, Culture, and Gender Binaries in Contemporary Australia*. U of Hawai'i P, 2006.

---. Introduction. *Boundary Writing: An Exploration of Race, Culture, and Gender Binaries in Contemporary Australia*, edited by Russell, U of Hawai'i P, 2006, pp. 1-17.

Samuels, Wilfred, et. al., editors, *Encyclopedia of African-American Literature*. Facts On File, 2007.

Sardar, Ziauddin. Foreword. *Black Skin, White Masks*, by Frantz Fanon, translated byCharles L. Markmann, Pluto, 2008, pp. vi-xx.

Secovnie, Kelly O. "Lorraine Hansberry (1930–1965)."Page, *Encyclopedia*, pp. 251-58.

Taylor III, Ordner W. "Harlem Renaissance." Page, *Icons of African American Literature*, pp. 103-32.

Sharon, Friedman. "Hansberry's Drama Rejects the Stereotype of the Emasculating Woman." Wiener, pp. 76-81.

Sickels, Amy. *African-American Writers: Multicultural Voices.* Chelsea-Infobase, 2010.

Singh, Amita. "A *Raisin in the Sun* Is Dominated by Women."Wiener, pp. 82-87.

Smith-Spears, RaShell R. "Black Arts Movement." Page, *Icons of African American Literature,* pp. 43-57.

Snodgrass, Mary Ellen. *Encyclopedia of Feminist Literature.* Facts on File-Infobase, 2006.

Walker, Alice. *In Search of Our Mothers' Gardens: Womanist Prose. Harvest-Harcourt, 1983.*

---. "Coretta King: Revisited" Walker, pp. 146-57.

---. "In Search of Our Mothers' Gardens." Walker, pp. 231-43.

Washington, Lynn. "Blues Aesthetic." Page,*Icons of African American Literature*, pp. 53-68.

West Traci C. "Extending Black Feminist Sisterhood in the Face of Violence: Fanon, White Women, and Veiled Muslim Women." Davidson et al., pp.157-82.

Wetmore Jr, and Howard A. Smith. *Suzan-Lori Parks: A Casebook*. Routledge, 2012.

Wiener, Gary, editor. *Social Issues in Literature: Gender in Lorraine Hansberry's A Raisin in the Sun.* Greenhaven Press, 2011.

Wilkerson, Margaret B. "Lorraine Hansberry: The Complete Feminist." Freedomways, 19.4 (1979), pp. 235-45.

---. Introduction. *Les Blancs: The Collected Last Plays* by Lorraine Hansberry, edited by Robert Nemiroff, Vintage Books, 1972, pp. 3-22.

Wisker, Gina, editor. *Black Women's Writing.* Macmillan Press, 1993.

---. *Post-Colonial and African-American Women's Writing:A Critical Introduction.* St. Martin's Press, 2000.

Wood, Jacqueline. "'Jazzing' Time, Love, and the Female Self in Three Early Plays." Kolin, pp. 34-44.

Woodworth, Christine. "Parks and the Traumas of Childhood." Kolin, pp. 140-55.

Young, Harvey. *Embodying Black Experience: Stillness, Critical Memory, and the Black Body*. U of Michigan P, 2010.

---. "Choral Compassion: In the Blood and Venus." Wetmore Jr., and Smith, pp. 29-47.

Young,Melvina Johnson. "Exploring the WPA narratives: Finding the voices of Black women and men." James and Busia, pp. 57-78.

3. Online Sources

"African American Literature." *En. Wikipedia. org.* Accessed29 June 2013. en.wikipedia.org/wiki/African-American_literature.

"Jupiter Hammon Biography." *Poem Hunter.com*. Accessed 25 June 2013. www.poemhunter.com/jupiter-hammon/biography/.

"Racism in the United States." *En. Wikipedia.org*. Accessed 7 Nov. 2013. en.wikipedia.org/wiki/Racism_in_the_United_States

"Social Justice Movements: Hansberry as a Social Activist." *Socialjustice. Ccnmtl. Columbia. Edu*. Accessed 1 Nov. 2013.

socialjustice.ccnmtl. columbia.edu/index.php/Han